MINDSHARING

THE ART OF
CROWDSOURCING
EVERYTHING

MINDSHARING

LIOR ZOREF

PORTFOLIO / PENGUIN

PORTFOLIO / PENGUIN

Published by the Penguin Publishing Group
Penguin Random House LLC
375 Hudson Street
New York, New York 10014

USA | Canada | UK | Ireland | Australia | New Zealand | India | South Africa | China
penguin.com
A Penguin Random House Company

First published by Portfolio / Penguin, an imprint of Penguin Publishing Group,
a division of Penguin Random House LLC, 2015

Illustration credits
Page 17: James Duncan Davidson / TED; 40 (two): Courtesy of the author; pages 59,
60 (two): LinkedIn Talent Blog; page 66: Rob Gunther; page 87: tpsdave, all-free
-download.com; page 100: Lance Deacon, tagxedo.com; page 187: Meir Pinto;
page 196: Moshe Tsoref; page 214: Ayala Tsoref; page 219: Jeff Pulver

LIBRARY OF CONGRESS CATALOGING-IN-PUBLICATION DATA
Zoref, Lior.
  Mindsharing : the art of crowdsourcing everything / Lior Zoref.
    pages cm
  Includes bibliographical references and index.
  ISBN 978-1-59184-665-9
  ISBN 978-1-59184-757-1 (export edition)
  1. Online social networks. 2. Decision making—Social aspects. 3. Group decision
making—Social aspects. 4. Problem solving—Social aspects. 5. Counseling—Social
aspects. 6. Social networks—Psychological aspects. I. Title.
  HM742.Z67 2015
  302.30285—dc23
                                        2014038642

Printed in the United States of America
10 9 8 7 6 5 4 3 2 1

Set in ITC New Baskerville Std
Designed by Neuwirth & Associates, Inc.

To my three children, Maya, Ori, and Assaf
And to the love of my life, Ayala

CONTENTS

PART 3

PART 4

MINDSHARING

INTRODUCTION: The Power of We

> Today, social networks are mostly about sharing moments. In the next decade, they'll also help you answer questions and solve complex problems.
>
> **MARK ZUCKERBERG, 2014**

L eo had a fever and a rash. His mother, Deborah, wasn't overly alarmed. Kids get sick all the time and fevers can come and go in a four-year-old boy. It was a Sunday and Mother's Day. The last thing Deborah wanted to do was spend the day in a waiting room, but she still dutifully took Leo to the pediatrician's office for an emergency visit.

From the waiting room, Deborah updated her Facebook status: *Nothing says Happy Mother's Day quite like a Sunday morning at the pediatrician.* After examining Leo, the doctor diagnosed strep and gave Leo a prescription for antibiotics. Deborah updated her status on Facebook once again. *Strep. No Biggie.*

A few days later, Leo's condition had worsened. The antibiotics didn't seem to be working, and as they waited for the results of yet another throat culture, Deborah took a picture of Leo looking miserable on the examining room table. She posted his photo on her Facebook wall and updated her status once again. *Baby getting sicker. Eyes swollen shut. Fever rising. Penicillin not working. Might be Scarlet fever. Or Roseola. Or . . . ???? Sigh.*

Deborah received many comments of support, and best wishes, and hopes for a speedy recovery for Leo. The next day she posted another picture of Leo, this time from home with his trusty stuffed bear at his side. This status read: *Swelling worse, especially eyes and chin. Fever still crazy high. Poor baby.*

Some people suggested he might have an allergy. Some said it must be scarlet fever. Others told her not to worry and offered hopes for a diagnosis soon. The crowd tried to provide their support as best they could. Many were parents themselves, and knew just how frightening it is to have your child sick and be helpless to do anything about it.

Soon after this last post, Deborah received a call from a Facebook friend who had been following her posts. Stephanie wasn't a doctor, but a mother, and she shared with Deborah that her son had had the exact same symptoms, and ended up being hospitalized for Kawasaki disease, a rare and often fatal illness. "You have to get to the hospital," Stephanie insisted. "The longer you wait, the worse the damage."

Deborah found her inbox filled with private messages. Two more Facebook friends, pediatricians, also suggested Kawasaki disease, and urged Deborah to take Leo to the hospital immediately.

In a little more than an hour, three different people suggested that Leo might have this very rare and fatal condition. Without having a name for it at the time, Deborah was engaging in Mindsharing. Deborah was turning to the wisdom of her crowd, her social network, and by her doing so, Leo's life was saved. In a blog post about her experience, Deborah wrote, "Was I consciously trying to find an answer out there in the hive mind? No, but some subconscious part of me must have been wondering whether one of my hundreds of 'friends' might be privy to some expertise on the befuddling Nutty Professor syndrome that had my child in its grips."

After rushing Leo to the hospital and confirming the diagnosis from her crowd, Deborah told the pediatrician about the crowd's diagnosing Kawasaki disease. His response? "Bravo Facebook." Deborah knew that her status updates, posted photos, and the collective wisdom of her crowd had saved her son's life.

Was Deborah's experience a fluke? Was it nothing more than a fortuitous mixture of fate and luck aligning at just the right time to save a four-year-old boy's life? Or had Deborah, by chance and by a mother's desperation, stumbled upon one of the most powerful resources available to us all?

MAKE BETTER DECISIONS

We all struggle to make the best decisions possible when it comes to our careers, finances, parenting, health, and relationships. But what if we could make every important decision with the help of the smartest people in the world? It might sound impossible, but it's not. All of us have the ability to access the collective wisdom of hundreds or even thousands of people who together are as smart as any expert adviser.

Making the right decisions is tough. Whenever we have an important decision to make, it can be difficult to put our feelings aside and make a rational and objective choice. Any emotion can affect our decision making, often long after the emotional incident has passed. A research study published by Eduardo Andrade and Dan Ariely shows that even "the influence of mild incidental emotions on decision making can live longer than the emotional experience itself."[1] What this means is that our decisions can be, and often are, fundamentally irrational or flawed. Andrade and Ariely's research shows that even a minor emotional incident can become the basis upon which we make future decisions. And the kicker is, we aren't even aware of it at the time. Someone cuts you off in traffic on your way to work and, much later in the day, you reject a business offer that's been in the works for weeks. You may not even think of the traffic incident ever again, but that fleeting annoyance, that surge of emotionally driven anger at the other driver, can affect your business decisions, or your personal decisions, and you won't even realize it.

When we reach out to the crowd for wisdom, we are able to access decision-making skills that are free of our own emotion. We are able to seek out the solutions to our problems and weigh our choices free of the bias intrinsic to unilateral decision making. If we learn to rely on and trust the wisdom of the crowd, our decisions will be better, quicker, and easier. There is a power in crowd wisdom, and this power is harnessed through technology and social media. The crowd (specifically, Aya Shapir, a young marketing professional in my crowd) has named this power "Mindsharing." And while it may sound like some futuristic version of a *Star Trek* Vulcan mind meld, it is a simple way to use the tools and technology already at hand to access and share our greatest human resource—one another.

Only this type of mind meld isn't limited to two minds.

It is important to note that when we Mindshare, we are not asking others to think *for* us, but rather, to think *with* us. And when others think with us it substantially improves our ability to make decisions and the quality of those decisions. I'm not saying that you surrender your free will and lay every future decision at the feet of the crowd, but through actively Mindsharing you can access the global brain (which is far more powerful than any individual brain) and hack your way into a better career, stronger relationships, and the fulfillment of virtually any dream or goal you can imagine.

NOT FOLLOWING THE HERD

Growing up I was taught that it is better to lead than to follow. Who has not heard their parents say, "If your friends jumped off a bridge, would you jump off one too?" We live in a time and a culture where great value is placed on individuality, on thinking for oneself independent of the herd. In the age of Mindsharing, there is a new paradigm to explore where greater value is placed on collective intelligence and collective problem solving. We are smarter as a group than we can ever be as individuals. In his 2004 book *The Wisdom of Crowds,* James Surowiecki argued that under certain conditions, the many are smarter than the few. The crux of crowd wisdom theory is that if you take a large crowd of people and ask them a question, their collective intelligence will be as smart as the answer of an expert.

Leveraging crowd wisdom through Mindsharing doesn't mean following the herd. It doesn't mean giving up our autonomy or independence. The crowd isn't making the decision, we are. But through the process of Mindsharing we gain access to information, insights, and knowledge that will improve our thinking and our lives dramatically. Make no mistake, Mindsharing is not groupthink. By definition, groupthink happens when a small group makes a faulty decision based on a misguided loyalty to the group or because the group is seeking harmony or conformity more than they are seeking truth. This conformity is often rationalized by a moral "rightness" to the belief system or values of the group. There is no diversity of opinion or dissenting voices when you have groupthink. By nature, groupthink does not invite independent thinking.

Mindsharing, however, can happen only *with* independent thinking, a diverse and heterogeneous group, and without any preformed belief in the "correct" decision or outcome. Crowd wisdom is the end result *only* when you have diverse and conflicting viewpoints that are generated by a large group of people of different ages, backgrounds, and areas of interest or expertise.

Mindsharing is the opposite of groupthink. It is a purposeful and pointed attempt to access the collective knowledge of humanity (or at least a large social network).

COLLECTIVE INTELLIGENCE

Have you ever witnessed a flock of birds flying in complete harmony? It is a sophisticated and synchronized ballet, but how do they do it? How do they know? How do honeybees decide in unison to move to a new nest? What about swarming ants? Schools of fish? Animals have a fascinating collective mind, and a collective decision-making process that has proven successful and ensured their survival.

When we make decisions or solve a problem, we are engaging in important cognitive processes. Mindsharing enhances our individual cognition or cognitive processes by utilizing the cognition of the crowd. Whenever the crowd solves a problem together, or makes a decision together, this is collective cognition, and the end result is collective intelligence.

In 2009, researcher and Princeton University professor Iain Couzin published findings about the group behavior of animals that demonstrated collective cognition.[2] He showed how animals use social interactions for collective decision making. For example, when honeybees need to choose a new nest, they send separate scouts to investigate potential nest locations.

When each scout returns, he does a dance for the other bees. This "waggle dance" communicates their recommendation. The longer the dance, the more enthusiastic they are about the nest. If the dance is convincing, more bees join and investigate the new nest, and return to dance alongside the original bee as a way to show consensus. This creates a positive feedback loop. At the end, the biggest dancing group prevails, and all the honeybees decide collectively that this is the best option for the group and as a group they move to their new nest.

What about humans? What could we accomplish if we had the same ability to tap into our collective minds and utilize our collective cognition?

In the past, if someone wanted to seek crowd wisdom, he or she would have to invest resources in order to find and interact with a big crowd. Today, many people have hundreds, and sometimes thousands, of social networking friends in their own crowd. If you are one of these people, you are lucky. You can use the collective intelligence of your friends when you have a pressing question that needs an expert answer. If you are not yet one of these people, don't despair—this book will teach you how to Mindshare with special Web sites and tools that you will be able to use, even if you have never seen a Facebook page in your life. If you update your status at every meal but only have your Grandma Jean and your two buddies from fifth-grade summer camp on your friends list, this book will also teach you how to grow your social network so that you can begin to utilize and benefit from Mindsharing.

Even if you regularly ask your social network for their opinion or help, this book will help you take this form of crowdsourcing to an entirely new level. Mindsharing happens when we make purposeful and directed attempts to access the collective intelligence of the crowd and harness this intelligence to make our lives and our world better. Just as the honeybees become what scientists call a "super-organism" when they use collective decision making, we too can become a super-organism when we Mindshare. There is power in turning to anyone, especially your friends, for help. But there is even more power when you turn to the friends of your friends—those outside your closest network and those you don't know very well and who don't know you very well. Sociology calls them our "weak ties."

In 1973, Professor Mark Granovetter from Johns Hopkins University published his paper "The Strength of Weak Ties."[3] His research explains why it is the weak ties in any social network that are the most important. Granovetter defines weak ties as acquaintances rather than close friends and family. For example, if you have two separate and distinct neighborhoods, or social networks, the only thing connecting them is their weak ties. If Joe knows Bob in neighborhood A, and Joe also knows Bill in neighborhood C, then Joe is the weak tie that connects the two neighborhoods and also the only connection between Bob and Bill. Granovetter explains that social networks that have more weak ties have the ability to coordinate more easily and make changes faster. Individuals with more weak ties (think of all those friends of friends on Facebook) also have faster mobility as well as greater access to resources. Weak ties are the bridges between us and any innovation or effective change we wish to make in our life. Weak ties are also where we get access to new information, novel ideas, and different areas of expertise. Our strong ties tend to be those who are most like us, but our weak ties are our link to the heterogeneity we need to Mindshare and access crowd wisdom.

In the book *Connected,* authors Nicholas Christakis and James Fowler[4] present research that confirms what Granovetter discovered in 1973—it is our weak ties that help us more than our strong ties. But what Christakis and Fowler also discovered is that while our strong ties, or immediate friends and family, have great impact on our personal lives, and even our health, our weak ties can also greatly affect us. For example, their research shows that an obese person has more friends who are obese. And also more friends of friends who are obese. And also more friends of friends of friends who are obese. And this network of obesity is too great to be attributed to chance or statistical probability. Here's the really shocking statistic: If you have an acquaintance or weak tie who becomes obese, it nearly triples your risk of becoming obese. Yes, the impact is greater if it is a strong tie—you have a 57 percent higher chance of obesity. But the risk is still high for the weak ties—20 percent higher with two degrees of separation and 10 percent higher with three degrees of separation.

This is just one example of the power of weak ties in our social networks. Our weak ties can also make us happier, wealthier, and more successful. Social economist James Montgomery studies weak ties and the role social networks play in the labor market. He found that weak ties are "positively related to higher wages and higher aggregate employment rates."[5]

So yes, your weak ties may make you obese, but they may also make you wealthier and more employed.

Your weak ties, your bridges to other networks and diverse groups, are the friends who will most profoundly influence your Mindsharing and create your access to collective intelligence.

Having access to collective intelligence is a very powerful asset. Just as the president always has his expert team of advisers by his side, you too can have wise advisers within reach whenever you are faced with a problem or dilemma that is beyond your own personal knowledge or expertise. You will learn how to build and manage digital relationships, and how Mindsharing can help you advance your career, improve your personal life, and coach you through achieving almost anything you can imagine. This is not rocket science. It is a simple way to tap into the full potential of your social network. You've heard the saying that two brains are better than one. What about five brains, fifty brains, five thousand brains? This book will guide you through the process.

THINKING WITH THE CROWD

Mindsharing is a crowdsourced thinking process to solve problems, make decisions, access creativity, and create more ease and joy in our lives. Instead of thinking alone, we use social technologies to think with a big crowd. The process involves asking questions, analyzing responses, and coming to an answer based on the collective wisdom of the crowd.

You may have heard of *crowdsourcing*, a term coined by Jeff Howe in 2005 as an alternative to outsourcing. Think of outsourcing as the process of giving a task to a third party. For example, a company might hire an advertising agency to create a marketing strategy. Outsourcing is a popular business tactic for organizations that are trying to focus on what they do best, and choose to outsource other tasks to professionals in that given area. Crowdsourcing, on the other hand, is the process of outsourcing a task to a large group of people (a crowd) rather than a professional or a single organization.

Wikipedia is without a doubt the largest and most well-known example of crowdsourcing, and in many ways the most important crowdsourcing effort thus far. It began on the premise that anyone in the world could offer valuable content, so anyone could add or edit information on a free online encyclopedia. Wikipedia is very extensive, but is it accurate? Can an unorganized, nonexpert crowd of volunteers provide correct information to the public without any supervision or guidance? In 2005, *Nature* magazine conducted a study in which experts analyzed forty-two articles from Wikipedia and *Encyclopaedia Britannica* to see which information source was more accurate. The study showed that the crowdsourced Wikipedia is nearly as accurate as the expert-created *Britannica*—independent experts found 3.9 errors per article in Wikipedia versus 2.9 errors per entry in *Encyclopaedia Britannica*. A later 2012 study, by Oxford University, found that Wikipedia articles scored higher than *Encyclopaedia Britannica* in accuracy.

Is the crowd getting even smarter?

Crowdfunding is another example of crowdsourcing. Instead of seeking out a single investor to fund a project with a large amount of money, crowdfunding seeks out a large group of people to invest a small amount each. After all, aren't a hundred investors better than one investor? What about ten million investors? Isn't it safer not to have all our eggs in one basket?

The traditional route for start-ups in need of capital is to go to a bank or a venture capital firm and pitch their idea in the hope that the one person behind the desk will believe in it enough to invest money. With crowdfunding, entrepreneurs can take their great and not-so-great ideas (the crowd will decide) directly to a huge audience of potential investors in order to get funding. Pebble Technology, a company developing smart watches that could display updates from a wearer's smart phone, went to Kickstarter seeking the seed money for their project. Originally, the company hoped to raise $100,000 by offering the watch at a discounted price to anyone who contributed $115 to the campaign. After only two hours postlaunch of their Kick-starter campaign, Pebble had raised the initial $100,000 they were seeking, and by the end of funding, less than forty days after going live with their project, they had well over $10 million. To date, Pebble is one of the most highly crowdfunded projects ever, with almost seventy thousand people contributing.

Both Wikipedia and Pebble are examples of organizations that are using the crowd. However, it took a big investment in time and resources to manage the crowdsourcing process. With Mindsharing, you can access the same powerful resource in your daily life and through your social networks. Instead of using your Facebook and Twitter accounts only to share your location, who you are with, what you are having for dinner, or your favorite cat video, you can use your networks in new, innovative, yet simple ways that will allow you to access the collective genius and power that resides in the brains of your friends, and in the friends of your friends, and so on across the globe. Deborah tapped into this intelligence to save her son's life. Countless others are tapping into it to invest their money, improve their career, find the love of their life, parent their children, and make impossible-seeming dreams come true.

This is Mindsharing, and it is different from traditional crowdsourcing because it is about crowdsourced thinking, not tasks—it is crowdsourced decision making. Mindsharing allows you to go to a big crowd and ask them to think *with* you. It bears repeating that Mindsharing is not about going to the crowd and asking them to think *for* you. It is tapping into the collective intelligence and power of the crowd, and using the crowd to help you make smarter decisions.

Now, you might wonder, "Aren't I Mindsharing every time I type a question into a search engine?" The answer is no. When you use a search engine, you are not asking people to think with you. You are using an algorithm that tries to find relevant information. In many cases, this information is from organizations that ultimately are trying to sell you something. For example, if you are trying to decide on the best place to go on vacation and you type this query into a search engine, you are going to get results from companies that are trying to get you to spend your money on whatever vacation paradise they are invested in.

With Mindsharing, however, your decision on the perfect vacation will be based on what you've said is valuable and relevant to you. There is no agenda with Mindsharing—you go to your crowd—and the expert advice is based on what you need, want, and value, not on what the crowd wants to sell you. Search engines are useful when looking for information or for facts and data, but they are less effective as a tool for decision making. Mindsharing isn't outsourcing your decision making. It's decision backup, and at its core it is all about innovation and novelty.

STATUS UPDATE

If you have ever switched careers, you know how important a decision it can be. This is why many of us invest so much time and effort in thinking about our career and usually seek the advice of our friends and family. Changing careers is right up there with life's other big decisions—getting married, starting a family, moving—and it is one of those decisions that have a long-term effect on our lives. When I first worked at Microsoft, I was very passionate about the (then) new social network revolution, and I had shared this passion with my crowd over the years. But the actual decision to leave Microsoft was made privately and with the advice and counsel of my family and a few close friends.

After deciding to make this life-changing career move and pursue a PhD, I had experimented with this thing called Mindsharing and been fascinated by the results. It was still a leap, however, to rely on the crowd to help me with my own decision making around my career and specifically my PhD research. My own cognitive process and intelligence, when it came to the question of what to do next in my life, left me lacking. I was unsure. I was worried about getting it wrong. I didn't even know what area of research to pursue for my PhD. It was then that I decided to get the advice of my crowd on Facebook and Twitter. Most of them knew what I did for a living, since I had often shared things from my professional life. So when I decided to retire from Microsoft, I wrote this status on my Facebook page:

What do you think should be my next career?

The response was overwhelming. The collective cognition of the crowd had processed all of my previous sharing about what I was passionate about in a way that I was not able to do on my own. The collective intelligence of the crowd not only ended up shaping my career, it ended up becoming my career. From a single status update, to a PhD, to consulting, to speaking engagements, to a TED talk, to this book—Mindsharing created my new career. The crowd's advice: create a career all about Mindsharing, and this is exactly what I do. I consult to organizations all around the world from health care to media to government agencies that want to use Mindsharing to make better decisions. But what I discovered was that organizations are not the only ones that benefit from crowdsourcing.

I used to ask myself, "Why do I need all these 'friends' on Facebook?" Most of them are more acquaintances than real friends. People I used to know in high school or from work. But after seeing their ideas, after Mindsharing with them, I finally understood that you never know the value and wisdom each of these friends has to offer.

I would soon need them more than I could ever have imagined.

HAVE YOU MET MY OX?

When I started to prepare my TED talk, I asked my crowd, "How do you think I can best create an 'Aha' moment for people to truly understand the idea of crowd wisdom and the power of Mindsharing? Bill Gates released mosquitoes during his talk. Jill Bolte Taylor showed a real human brain. What should I do?"

I received many ideas, some bad and some good. Then, sixteen-year-old Or Sagy suggested that I recreate the most famous crowd wisdom experiment from more than a hundred years ago. The experiment he was referencing (and how did a sixteen-year-old know this?) was originally published in 1907 by Francis Galton in the journal *Nature*.[6] At a crowded country fair in Plymouth, England, Galton held a contest where he had eight hundred people guess the weight of a slaughtered and dressed ox. The crowd, where no one individually knew the weight of a dead ox, collectively guessed the weight of the ox when their individual guesses were tallied and the median weight determined. The collective intelligence of this crowd was also more accurate than any of the estimates of cattle experts that were solicited separately from the crowd.

Or wasn't suggesting I butcher an ox, but instead that I bring a real ox onstage and let the TED crowd guess the ox's weight. Initially, I thought that this was a crazy idea. A real ox? Come on . . . But here's the thing about crowd wisdom: the crowd judges its own intelligence. Many people saw the ox recommendation and thought it was a great idea. Suddenly, everyone told me, "Ask for an ox!"

I was nervous and a bit unsure. How does someone go about asking for an ox? I decided to put my trust in the crowd and wrote an e-mail to the TED team about my plans for my talk. At the end of this e-mail I wrote, "So, can I have an ox, please?" I pressed "Send" and then I waited. An hour passed by—no response. Another hour went by, still no response. I went to sleep that night, and had my first (of many) TED nightmares. In my dream, the TED team receives my e-mail and convenes an urgent meeting to discuss how "This Lior guy is really losing it!" They are all sitting in the meeting room, and decide to inform me that they are sorry, but I can't speak at TED. The ox thing was just too crazy, and they were crazy to consider me worthy of speaking at TED.

I woke up just as the TED team in my dream was saying, "Sorry, but don't call us, we will call you." I immediately ran to my computer to check my mail, and much to my surprise, there was a response telling me that *they loved* this idea, and they would do their best to find me an ox. I was surprised, excited— and afraid all over again. What if someone sitting in the front row wears a red dress and the ox decides to charge? What if the ox drinks too much water and decides to relieve itself onstage? There were many sleepless nights as I envisioned every catastrophe imaginable associated with giving a TED talk with an ox. I was doomed, and all because I had the brilliant idea to listen to the crowd and bring an ox onstage during my TED talk.

Two weeks later I was notified that the TED team had reached out to a company that delivers animals to Hollywood movies. Not only did I have an ox, I had a movie-star ox. I had the Tom Cruise of oxen.

When the ox came onstage, my heart skipped a beat. I breathed heavily and started to walk toward him. He was behaving exactly the opposite of how he had behaved in my nightmares. He seemed relaxed and like he was having a great time. This ox was a true professional.

I put my hand on his back and welcomed him to TED. Then, I asked the audience to guess his weight and send their estimate using their smart phones. The audience started to type their guesses into their phones, as I continued with my talk. Suddenly the ox began to stare at a woman in the audience who happened to be wearing a red dress. I suggested to her that a red dress might not have been the best choice she could have made, and while the audience cheered, I thought, *I hope TED has an insurance rider that covers a rampaging ox.*

Then it was time for my moment of truth. There were more

than five hundred estimates from the crowd. The lowest was 308 pounds. The highest was 8,004 pounds. Who thinks that an ox weighs 8,000 pounds? (Apparently four different people in the audience did.) When I was handed the envelope on the TED stage, I was so happy and relieved to see the results. The ox's real weight was 1,795 pounds and the average from the crowd was 1,792 pounds. No single person knew the weight of that ox, but together the crowd was as smart as any ox farmer in America. Crowd wisdom worked a hundred years ago, it worked for me on the TED stage, it worked for me in creating this book, and it can work in your life as well.

Let's begin our exploration of what is possible when you tap into the power of Mindsharing.

MINDSHARING
FOR YOUR CAREER
AND YOUR SUCCESS

1.

FINDING YOUR CROWD
(Building the New Network)

I t was my last day at Microsoft. After fourteen wonderful years, I was leaving my position as a vice president of marketing in order to start my PhD. I was scared. Among the many forms that human resources provides when you go through a "separation" is the dreaded *Exit Form*. This form contained a list of all the Microsoft assets I had to return. I dutifully went down the list—returning my laptop, my desktop, my cell phone, the key to my office, my SIM card, and my company car. It was only after returning the car that it became painfully clear I hadn't thought through my last day at Microsoft very well—I realized I had no way to get home.

With each item I returned, I felt the loss more profoundly. It wasn't as though I defined myself by my Microsoft assets, but they had been a part of my professional identity for so many years. During my career, I had become more and more known by the moniker "Lior from Microsoft," and now I was becoming just "Lior" again. I wondered about the loss I felt. Would I still be a professional without the pieces of my professional life? I experienced a mini existential crisis as I let go of my laptop, my cell phone, my office key, and my company car. It is hard to find a job, yes, but it can be harder still to walk away from a job. There was a certain security in each of those "assets" I had to return. As I stepped into the elevator for the last time, I felt bereft and confused. Had I just turned in my entire career? My future? My expertise?

I pressed the ground floor button and felt my stomach drop right along with the elevator. Did I have anything left I could call my own professionally? I reviewed the exit form in my head, feeling as if I had forgotten something important. Something critical. It was then that I realized there was no line item on that form asking me to turn over my Facebook friends, or my Twitter followers, or my LinkedIn connections. I hadn't handed over everything to Microsoft. My single most important professional asset did not belong to any corporation—it belonged to me.

I still had my network.

I still had my crowd.

IF YOU BUILD IT, THEY WILL COME

We are programmed to be smart in a new way—a way that produces intelligence. In his book *The Wealth of Networks*, Harvard professor Yochai Benkler calls this "social production," a new production model in a networked society. His theory shows how society no longer needs to rely only on industrial or organized production because connected crowds can produce value in a completely new way. Building on his ideas, Mindsharing offers a new production model for human intelligence in the age of social networking. Professor Benkler predicts that social production is not just a trend, but the most critical economic and cultural shift that will transform society.

When we rely on the collective intelligence of the crowd through Mindsharing, we can make decisions that are better, wiser, and of greater value. Success, in any area, can come just as readily from thinking cooperatively as it does from thinking competitively. Some may even suggest it comes more readily. In order to tap into the wisdom of your own personal crowd, however, you first have to build that crowd.

If you are an existing Facebook user, how big is your crowd? Look at your friends list. Do you have three friends or three thousand friends? To Mindshare you need at least 250 friends. Why this number? In 2010, researchers Christian Wagner and Tom Vinaimont from City University of Hong Kong published their evaluation of crowd wisdom and attempt to validate the findings (scientifically rather than anecdotally) that a crowd could guess or estimate a number more accurately than an expert.[1] They found that an expert could outperform a small crowd of nonexperts, but a large crowd of nonexperts could outperform the expert. Their analysis compared a crowd of 30 people with a crowd of 999 people and found that "based on simulation results, a crowd of 30 competing against a 10-times more precise expert would statistically outperform the expert in about 38% of all cases, while a crowd of 999 under the same conditions should have an 89% win ratio." The crowd of 30 proved to perform quite well when asked to estimate the number of candies in a container.

So how do I get from 30 to 250 as the minimum number of crowd size to effectively Mindshare? Facebook research shows that an average status update or post reaches 12 percent of that person's friends or followers. If you are Mindsharing and you need a minimum of 30 responses to get crowd wisdom (999 is even better), then you need 250 friends (250 × 12% = 30). It's not an exact calculation, but it is the minimum number I have found (and research has proven) will give good results when Mindsharing. It's about the number of people in your network, and also the number of people who are engaging with you. Not everyone who sees a Mindshare will respond. If your question is not interesting, or your friends sense a hidden agenda in your question, it doesn't matter how big your network—you won't get the results you're looking for. We will discuss this more in Part Two: The Art of Mindsharing. For now, it is important to know that you could have 3,000 friends but if they are not engaged with you, you won't have a crowd suitable for Mindsharing.

As a beginner, the general rule is at least 250 friends to Mindshare. If your list is not that big, get busy building your crowd by sending out friend requests. Look at whom Facebook naturally suggests you add as a friend based on your mutual connections, your location, your education, your place of employment. Facebook can discern your closest and most logical crowd based on these criteria, but you can also search out those you would like to include in your crowd. As you build your crowd, you are building a successful foundation for Mindsharing. Remember, to get the wisdom of any crowd it needs to be both big enough and diverse enough (varied ages, gender, location, etc.). When it is both, you will be able to use the intelligence of this crowd to potentially solve big problems, make better decisions, and even fulfill your dreams.

The upside to Mindsharing with your Facebook crowd is that you always have an option to Mindshare with your own crowd. While not every Facebook friend is your best friend, each has his or her own value to give. In addition, each one usually knows you well enough to help you think and to help you make decisions.

The potential downside to Mindsharing with your Facebook crowd is that it is not anonymous. If your boss is friends with you on Facebook, this might not be the place to Mindshare that you've always hated your job and are looking for a new career. In this case, there are anonymous places online for Mindsharing for those times when you do not want your crowd to consist of your immediate friends, family, or colleagues. We will discuss these anonymous sites in later chapters, but one of them is worth mentioning now—Quora. Quora (www.quora.com) is a community with more than a million and a half monthly users asking questions covering more than four hundred thousand topics. Quora is the leading question-and-answer platform, where people are enthusiastic about asking and answering questions. The people responding to questions may or may not be experts on a particular topic, but each usually does believe he or she has knowledge to share. When asking a question, you can choose to remain anonymous or post using your real name. Each question can relate to specific topics. Other Quora users who follow these topics are able to read and respond. Just as on Facebook, users can "follow" one another on Quora.

Want to know exactly how one goes about joining a circus at your age? Quora will have the answer, and no one close to you (and certainly not your boss or your spouse) ever needs to know you asked the question.

MAKING A REAL CONNECTION WITH YOUR CROWD

When you share something with the crowd, or ask for help from the crowd, there is a certain vulnerability involved in the asking regardless of whether you are asking your strong ties or your weak ties. There is a very real fear of oversharing within a culture of transparency. Our most valuable currency when we are Mindsharing is our ability to be authentically ourselves. We are all human, struggling, growing, learning, trying, and failing. The more we can share our humanity with the crowd, the more engaged our crowd will be. The crowd has a low interest in PR and a high interest in real human emotions. This is why most of us are uninterested in advertising and riveted by dramatic stories.

Social media has often been driven by a need to project a certain image and a certain "status" to the world. Look at my happy family. See my beautiful vacation photos. Look how much my partner publicly expresses his or her love for me. Congratulate me on my work promotion. Buy my product.

Mindsharing is not about comparing what's on the outside, but about authentic sharing of what's on the inside. It's about relying on one another and leaning on one another in business and in our personal life in ways that are based on genuine connection and shared value. We may read someone's status about which luxury sedan to buy, and move on from this "Cadillac problem" without responding. But when we come across a genuine Mindshare—where someone is scared about changing careers and asking for advice, or feeling lonely and wanting to meet someone—we resonate with that vulnerability and openness and we want to connect and give value back. The same is true for whatever we choose to share. We all intuitively know when something or someone is real, and we also know when something or someone is manipulative and false.

Vulnerability is powerful. And it takes courage to be vulnerable. Perhaps you are sharing that you are looking for more meaning and purpose in your life or in your career. It can be a bit frightening. I promise you, though, for every genuine question you pose to your crowd, for every genuine thought you share, what you get back from the collective wisdom of that crowd will make it worth it ten times over. After reading this book, give it a shot. Try it out with your crowd. Start small and work your way up. I was afraid to leave my job at Microsoft. I was afraid to share my dream of one day speaking at TED. Of writing a book. Every fear or doubt I have ever shared with the crowd has been lessened by the crowd. In the end, the crowd will always have your back.

LOCATION, LOCATION, LOCATION

As you've already learned through Quora, Facebook is not the only real estate in town when it comes to Mindsharing. Twitter, LinkedIn, Google+, and personal blogs are without a doubt the most common and well-known platforms for Mindsharing. Each has its pros and cons. You may choose to keep your personal and professional Mindsharing activities distinct and separate, or you may wish to commingle them as I do. Unlike Facebook, LinkedIn is typically used to create a professional network and connect with existing and potential business partners. You may wish to utilize your Facebook crowd for personal Mindsharing and your LinkedIn crowd strictly for your career and business. We will discuss LinkedIn in more detail in chapter 4, including how to search out and join relevant professional groups and Mindshare among experts. For now, here is a quick, down-and-dirty cheat sheet for Mindsharing Locales where you may want to build your crowd.

Facebook

WHAT IT'S GOOD FOR:

- If you have a big crowd, Facebook lends itself to any kind of Mindsharing you can dream up.

- Your crowd is always there and ready to think with you.

- There are also groups for unique areas of interest where there is a highly engaged and specialized crowd eager to Mindshare on those topics.

PROS:

- If you're an active Facebook user, it is the most convenient and immediate way to Mindshare.

- Your Facebook friends know you and care about you so they are invested in coming up with solutions for you.

CONS:

- You need to have at least 250 friends. If your crowd is not big enough or diverse enough, your responses will not reflect the collective wisdom of a crowd.

- No anonymity. Mindsharing on Facebook is equivalent to standing naked in front of a crowd. In this case (hopefully) we are talking about being emotionally naked and therefore vulnerable. For very professional questions, you might prefer to keep your clothes on and Mindshare with a different crowd.

LinkedIn

WHAT IT'S GOOD FOR:

- Mindsharing among experts.

PROS:

- If you have a professional question, LinkedIn groups are the best places to Mindshare among experts.

- Even if you are not active on Facebook, you can still access a large crowd and Mindshare within targeted groups in your areas of interest.

CONS:

- There is a time investment involved in searching out and joining relevant professional groups.

- Some groups are quite large, and your question may not be visible for a long enough time to get the number of responses you need for Mindsharing.

Twitter

WHAT IT'S GOOD FOR:

- Short, quick, easy-to-understand questions that your crowd can respond to in an equally short response (up to 140 characters).

PROS:

- The fastest way to Mindshare—responses happen immediately. Closest to real-time Mindsharing.

CONS:

- It is difficult to Mindshare in 140 characters or less if your question or decision is complex.

- As with Facebook, you need at least a few hundred followers to make up your crowd.

Quora

WHAT IT'S GOOD FOR:

- Complicated or tough questions that require a very large crowd.

PROS:

- It is one of the largest platforms available for group thinking.

- You can stay anonymous. You do not need to involve your Facebook friends or Twitter followers.

CONS:

- As in LinkedIn groups, you need to ask your questions in an interesting or provocative way in order to get answers from this large community. Unlike questions posed to your Facebook friends (who have a closer relationship to you and may even be willing to respond to your most boring question), questions on Quora that do not interest the crowd will not get a response from the crowd.

Google+

WHAT IT'S GOOD FOR:

- Mindsharing similar to what you would do on Facebook. Also lends itself to detailed questions requiring detailed answers.

PROS:

- Usually a bit more business oriented than Facebook, but with a smaller and more personal crowd.

- Good for tech questions, and users are usually quite enthusiastic.

CONS:

- At this time, it is difficult to gather a crowd large enough for Mindsharing.

- Not anonymous.

Blog Writing

WHAT IT'S GOOD FOR:

- Telling your story in a consistent and more detailed way, and Mindsharing where you offer more of who you are and what you are passionate about.

PROS:

- It's the best way to give value to a big audience, and you are not limited to time or word constraints.

- Your blog post cannot get lost in a news feed, and it stays searchable for a long time compared with other formats.

CONS:

- Time-consuming. It takes considerable time to write and manage an active blog and requires a bigger time investment from the crowd to read.

- It's challenging and takes time to build a crowd of dedicated readers who are committed to Mindsharing.

Whether you build your crowd on Facebook or Twitter, find your crowd on LinkedIn or Quora, or begin writing a blog and build your crowd from there—the important thing is to have a large crowd that wants to Mindshare with you and will respond to the questions you ask. This is your valuable asset. As technology changes very fast, there are always new and updated platforms to use. If you'd like to get an updated list of these platforms, including examples of how to use them, please visit mindsharing.info/locales.

You have to get the crowd to join you. They have to be invested in your life, personal or career. This goes back to the vulnerability we mentioned earlier. The crowd is only going to join you and be invested if you are genuine—a real person with real struggles just like them. And a big part of being genuine is being vulnerable. You have to get the crowd to care.

How do you do all this?

Create value for the crowd.

ONLY ONE LESSON

When I started out as a marketing manager at Microsoft, I knew very little about marketing. My experience was in computer programming. I knew how to write code. My only previous experience with marketing was while playing in a very bad high school rock band. We spent two long months making and hanging posters to promote our one big show. The end result—an audience of ten people who had nowhere else to be.

Almost thirty years later, there are still high school rock bands, but posters have gone the way of the rotary telephone. Today kids are digital natives and they can create a fan page on Facebook, seed the audience with YouTube videos, share pictures to promote the show on Instagram, and register and track their potential audience in real time.

There is one thing that hasn't changed in thirty years or with the advent of social media, and it is exactly what my very first boss told me was the only thing I needed to know about marketing: *be unforgettable.*

How was I supposed to do this? He told me that I needed to plan activity after activity with and for my business partners. This meant endless planning and execution of training seminars, comarketing activities, golf tournaments, speaking engagements, and always mailing them brochures and product promotions and other marketing materials. This is how I would make my company unforgettable to them, and whenever a potential business opportunity arrived, they would call Microsoft. They would be invested. It was a time-consuming endeavor, but my boss wasn't crazy, he was absolutely right.

This lesson is as important to successful Mindsharing as it is to successful marketing. In Mindsharing you become unforgettable by providing value to your crowd, and always reminding your crowd who you are and what you stand for. Whether you are marketing a brand or building your crowd, you want others to remember you. Seventeen years ago, before Facebook or Twitter or YouTube, being unforgettable meant constant face-to-face engagements with business partners. It meant dinners, events, and sales calls. In the digital age, in Mindsharing, it means something a little different.

It still means constant engagement with people, but it is about engaging people in real conversations, not promotional activities or sales pitches. Whether you are promoting your business, promoting your brand, or promoting yourself, you need to not just build a crowd but also engage a crowd in a positive way. You have to be honest. You may have to be a bit vulnerable. If you want your crowd to spend time with you, to Mindshare with you, you have to be real in order to create real value.

Value is the key. When you give value through social media it means that what you share educates, or inspires, or helps people do their job better, or aids them in their personal life. Value is making someone laugh, think, or feel. Giving value will build your crowd, so every time you Mindshare, when you engage your crowd or network, ask yourself what value you are adding. When it comes to your career, value is more important than an embossed business card or a promotional picture of you on the side of a bus or the back of a shopping cart. It may even be more important than the words on your résumé. Whatever your profession or whatever your passion—when you give value to people they will follow you, they will remember you, and if you are looking for a new career or for career advancement, they will hire you. When you create value, you create an engaged crowd. And as you will learn throughout this book, when you have an engaged crowd, you can achieve almost anything.

WHERE CAN I GET SOME VALUE?

Value can be anything. It can be something you write, a link to an article or video you find interesting, an intriguing question you pose, or some other information you share that means something to you and to your life. When you share something that has value for you, it will create value for your crowd. Value can be something that makes people laugh, makes people cry, or makes people marvel at the mystery of life. Value in Mindsharing also relates to more practical things—helping people get what they want, or saving someone time by sharing your knowledge, information, and experience. Value is subjective, of course, but value is usually not a cat video or a picture of what you are having for dinner. Value is also a two-way street. Giving value is just that: giving. It's not about public relations or selling people a product. It is about making people think. It's about making people feel. It's a clear belief and a clear point of view. You will know that what you share has value by the response you get from your crowd. Do they like your post, do they share your post, do they engage with the idea or question in your post (or blog or tweet)? Do they add to the conversation, and bring others in their network into the conversation? When you provide value (in all its many forms), your crowd will grow. It may be a gradual growth, but constantly over time, if you give value, you will become unforgettable. And the number one lesson in marketing and in Mindsharing is: *be remembered.* If you are genuine in sharing who you are and what you are interested in, your

crowd will respond, engage, follow you, and invite others to follow you as well. If you care, the crowd will care. It takes time
and effort to engage the crowd and make them care, but when
the crowd cares, the superpowers of Mindsharing are yours to
command.

2

THE NEW NETWORK

(Mindsharing Your Career)

My three-year-old son, Ori, is reading the newspaper. I see him from across the room, holding the paper oddly and staring intently at the front page. Now Ori, genius that he is, cannot yet read. I move closer to him and see there is a picture of a cat on the front page. Ori loves cats, but he seems extremely unhappy and frustrated with this particular cat.

"It's not working!" he says sadly, holding the paper up for me to see.

I am confused for a moment, until he shows me.

"Daddy," he cries, as he repeatedly presses his little finger against the cat's face. "The newspaper is not working!"

This is our new world. And in this new world, for every newspaper reader who dies, there will be no replacement born. For Ori, for an entire generation growing up right now, digital interaction isn't the exception, but the norm. Now some of you may not like this. Some of you may even long for times gone by—the "good ol' days" when newspapers weren't expected to have pictures that come to life. Lamenting days gone by, however, does not prepare us for a future that is already here. Ori expects pictures to move when he touches them, to speak to him when he speaks to them, and for all his learning, efforts, and decision making, to be in real time and in cooperation and collaboration.

In short, Ori, and an entire generation of "digital natives," is already prepared for Mindsharing.

Are we?

NO MORE CLASSIFIEDS

It used to be that looking for a job (or a job change) involved sitting at the kitchen table with the classifieds section of the newspaper in front of you, circling possibilities. It meant writing a résumé, printing it out, drafting a cover letter, and mailing it off to anonymous faces in human resources. Or it meant endless hours pounding the pavement, newspaper in hand, only to find that jobs that were placed in the Sunday newspaper ahead of printing deadlines were already filled by the time you walked in the door. Finding a job this way was the equivalent of Ori's pressing on the cat's face in the newspaper and thinking it would come to life. Overall, it was a cumbersome and frustrating endeavor, and finding a job felt much like a crapshoot or a game of chance. Would you be lucky enough to be at the right place at the right time?

Today, in the digital age and with the power of your crowd, career placement or advancement is not a matter of luck or spending fruitless hours trying to be at the right place at the right time. Every critical decision you make can be made with the help of Mindsharing. Every important bit of information—from secret salaries to unpublished job openings—is available. Even résumés and business cards can be created with minimal effort when you harness the collective power of the crowd. Mindsharing is revolutionizing the ways we seek employment and pursue our dream jobs. It is also transforming the way employers find and hire prospective employees. Obtaining a job may always feel a bit overwhelming—frustrating even—but when you rely on the crowd and tap into current technology and digital networks to help, the job of finding a job is much easier.

After I left Microsoft, I had to design new business cards. I was no longer "Lior from Microsoft." Today, I believe that business cards are mostly a waste of time. Your blog, your LinkedIn profile (which we'll discuss in the next chapter), and your Twitter account are more important than any business card. But back then, I needed a new card to reflect my career change.

I am no graphic designer, but I decided not to hire a professional. Instead, I turned to my network, the crowd I had taken with me when I departed Microsoft. I shared a simple draft of a potential business card with my Facebook friends and posted this as my status: "What do you think should be on my business card?"

After only a few hours, I received many great ideas from my crowd. They helped me to create a clean and beautiful business card that I could never have come up with by myself or without spending a lot of money. More important than the design of the card, however, was the content of my new business card. I received many great ideas about smart ways to share my social-networking and digital presence on my business card. The crowd came up with the brilliant ideas to add a QR code and a place to write a comment, just like on Facebook.

Designing a business card with my crowd was one of my earliest Mindsharing experiences. The end result was, in my opinion, as great as any expert in graphic design could have created. Something else spectacular happened, however, when I Mindshared this small part of my career—my crowd became engaged and interested in my new career path. They were part of it now, and my success would become their success. We were in it together, and neither I, nor my crowd, had any idea just how far we would go.

Here is what my new business card looked like (minus the color and my phone numbers and address).

Front

Back

A better business card isn't the only way to Mindshare for your career. Let's tackle the dreaded résumé. Résumés aren't easy. Do you list your jobs in reverse chronological order? Do you list your skills or your experience first? What about outside interests? How do you complete the tough "Objective" portion of the résumé, other than to say your objective is to get this particular job right now? Former senator Bob Bennett calls a résumé "a written exaggeration of only the good things a person has done in the past, as well as a wish list of the qualities a person would like to have."

I couldn't have said it better.

There are thousands of Web sites with samples and tips on writing a winning résumé. Most of these tips are generic, all-purpose, and, frankly, outdated. Some of them give you a free template to complete, and after spending hours filling in the information for your résumé, you find you can only print or save it by paying a fee, or becoming a member of that particular site. But you already have the only membership you will ever need—you belong to your new network, your crowd. No fees required.

Writing a great résumé won't happen by following generic tips from an anonymous résumé site; you need tips specific to *your* résumé and *your* job search. With Mindsharing, there are many ways to create the perfect résumé. If you are open enough, you can do as I did with my business card, and post your résumé on Facebook and ask your friends for their feedback. If you wish to get more private assistance (and I can understand why), you can post your résumé anonymously to one of the many crowdsourcing Web sites that have specific areas of interest for résumés. You can Mindshare your résumé without anyone knowing your identity.

Reddit is one example of a Web site (www.reddit.com/r /resumes) that has a unique "subreddit" or area of interest called "résumés." You can post your résumé into a Google document or any other file-sharing service and then post a link at Reddit asking people to critique, help, or do something more specific. Here are some examples of Mindsharing posts on Reddit:[1]

- I'm having trouble landing jobs. Could you take a look at my résumé?

- Trying to get a job in Web development, would love your merciless critique on this résumé!

- I'm writing my first real résumé and don't have a lot of experience.

- Do you put skills you don't have on your résumé?

- I can bullshit my way through anything. How can I put this on my résumé?

That last question is one of my personal favorites, and you are not likely to find the answer to that on a generic job or résumé-building Web site.

Another good site for résumé Mindsharing is Quora. There is a unique topic at Quora called "Résumé and CV Writing." Here, you can get experts (or people passionate about writing résumés) to answer your résumé questions and offer solutions. I recently saw a résumé question answered by the general manager at Amazon. My personal favorite was a question that a Quora user posted asking people, "What is the craziest thing you've ever seen or written in a résumé?" An owner of a company responded with this:

I actually had a candidate put this on his résumé. I strongly considered interviewing him just to meet him.

Objective: To dive into a swimming pool of gold coins like Scrooge McDuck

Now you might not want to put this on your résumé, but Mindsharing not only can provide specific answers to your questions, it can open the door to new ideas and ways of thinking "outside the box." Maybe putting something obscure or humorous on your résumé is just the way to get an interview for a more creative-type job, and maybe you would never have thought of this without Mindsharing.

BRING THE WATERCOOLER TO YOU

One of the more challenging aspects of job searching and interviewing is the question of salary. You've probably been asked in an interview, "What are your salary requirements?" It's a stress-provoking question. What if I ask for too much and they don't hire me? What if I ask for too little and they don't hire me? Or what if they hire me and I could have been paid more?

It used to be that salaries were highly guarded secrets within an organization. Not any longer. Glassdoor (www.glassdoor .com) is an inside look at jobs and companies. You can find out what it's really like to work at a particular company, for a particular CEO, and also what people are getting paid.

At Glassdoor, people are providing real insight into what corporate life and corporate culture are all about in any given workplace. You don't have to take the company's view on what it's like as gospel, you can reach out to the crowd and get the real deal. It's like having a personal friend who works where you want to work giving you the watercooler gossip firsthand.

Glassdoor is to job seekers what TripAdvisor is to travelers. Every company recruiter might tell you that "employees love working here," but sites like Glassdoor will give you the truth, not the company line. For example, according to Glassdoor, Facebook employees are satisfied with their corporate culture by a score of 4.5 out of 5. Google comes in at 4.2, Apple at 3.9, and Microsoft at 3.6.[2]

The most anxiety-provoking part of any job search is the interview. The crowd at Glassdoor not only can ease your interview anxiety, they can tell you exactly what questions they were asked during their interview by whatever specific company you are researching.[3] Want to know how Apple interviews its potential employees? Curious as to the hiring process at American Express? Did your Google search of Google turn up nothing of value you can take with you on your interview? Glassdoor is a great example of how Mindsharing is making organizations more transparent, whether they like it or not, and saving candidates a lot of time and guesswork and sleepless nights planning their next career move.

NO EXPERIENCE REQUIRED

If you are new to the job market or new to a particular field, the old adage says, "You can't get a job without experience, and you can't get experience without a job." It's a classic catch-22 and has stymied many seeking to enter the job market or seeking a career change to an entirely different field. Mindsharing solves this dilemma, and gives you new ways to gain experience in your chosen field. Past experience is often the critical factor for hiring managers in determining who they will call in for an interview and ultimately hire. So unless you plan to lie on your résumé, what do you do?

More and more companies and small businesses are using the crowd to complete tasks, problem solve, and innovate. And more people are joining crowd-based marketplaces to gain experience and build résumés and portfolios.

Do you have a particular skill? A unique talent? Check out Fiverr (www.fiverr.com). Billed as the world's largest marketplace for services (most being sold for five dollars each), Fiverr lets you sell your skills to the crowd while building up your résumé and gaining new skills and experience that can help you land a more permanent position that is asking for more qualifications than you currently have. One Web site designer is offering to design a four-page Web site for five dollars. Perhaps you're professionally trained or self-taught as a video editor. You can offer to edit video or create video for five dollars. You won't get rich, but your résumé will be full of relevant experience and client references. You can also go to this site and find people who will edit your résumé and design your business card for only five dollars.

Marcus Halbig loves to play with chain saws. He is forty-three years old and has been juggling chain saws for more than twenty years. It used to be that as a street performer his only way of getting paid was by performing on the street. Not a great gig if you live in the Pacific Northwest where it rains all the time (chain saws are very slippery when wet). Marcus decided to join the crowd at Fiverr and sell his unique talent online. For five dollars, Marcus will produce and create a custom video in which he juggles either two sharp knives or, for an additional fee, a chain saw (with the blade running). He juggles while reciting or singing text the buyer provides him. Believe it or not, Marcus's digital street performance is hugely popular, and he earns enough to support himself full-time.

Whether you wish to earn extra income, broaden your skills, or build an amazing client portfolio in five-dollar increments, the crowdsourced model of Fiverr is an innovative way to participate in the online job community and economy.

ALGORITHMS AND INNOVATION

Mindsharing can help you gain experience as an employee, but companies are also turning to Mindsharing to find employees, fill positions, and solve some of their biggest corporate challenges. When it comes to employment opportunities, Mindsharing is a two-way street.

When I was in high school, I got my first real job (helping my mom around the house didn't count). I worked at a computer retail store during my school vacation. I was a geek from the time I could walk and talk, and since I loved computers so much I thought that selling them would be fun. I also wanted to earn money so I could buy the things I saw other kids, *popular* kids, wearing.

Those were the early days in the personal computer industry. I started out selling Apple II computers, and then the IBM PCs and compatible computers (you're welcome, Steve Jobs and Bill Gates). Each and every time I made a successful sale of one of these computers, I felt an adrenaline rush.

One of my earliest lessons from the store manager was about upselling and cross-selling. Upselling is offering additional products to add to the original sale, and cross-selling is offering additional products that the customer might want based on their purchase profile. It's similar to the waiter asking you if you'd like a dining membership card (cross-selling) and then offering you a beautiful apple pie for dessert (upselling).

The objective, of course, was to increase the final sale amount. In addition to computers, I found myself selling tutorial software packages (that I developed), computer covers, and even specialized PC desks. Now it's hard to imagine that we used to need a huge table just to use a PC and monitor. It was time-consuming work—upselling and cross-selling—but it got the job done and made my employer extremely happy.

Today, many upselling and cross-selling activities are done digitally through complex algorithms that attempt to predict other products you might be interested in based on your purchases. Whenever you buy a product on Amazon, you get recommendations for other products that you might like and a snapshot of what other customers purchased who purchased the same book, music, or other product that you did. The same happens when you watch a movie on Netflix, and with activities on countless other Web sites.

These recommendations have a big impact on sales. This is why online retailers invest heavily in trying to improve the performance of their algorithms. In 2009, Netflix opened a competition for those who could come up with the best recommendation algorithm. It offered a prize of one million dollars to whoever could create an algorithm with better results than Netflix's existing one. The winning team managed to improve Netflix's own algorithm results by more than 10 percent. Customers were able to get better recommendations for movies they would be interested in, and Netflix was able to increase its sales and profits.

Most businesses believe that the biggest and best ideas come from a few clever brains working in-house. These could be inspired founders, visionary CEOs, or any other senior leader in charge of "innovation" for a company. Yet as we see repeatedly, Mindsharing creates group genius that achieves better results, especially in cases where breakthrough innovation or problem solving is needed.

There are many crowdsourcing platforms that can help businesses and nonprofits to tap into the power of Mindsharing by having a big and diverse crowd solve a problem for them. One of the leading platforms is InnoCentive (www.innocentive .com). It has a community with more than 300,000 registered people who are passionate about problem solving, and a reach that exceeds thirteen million. InnoCentive allows businesses and nonprofits to post cash prizes for solutions to challenges, and then brokers the exchange of intellectual property and prize between solver and challenger.

InnoCentive has a success rate of 85 percent in its challenges and believes that innovation truly happens when you don't rely on one individual or department or company to solve a problem. In short, InnoCentive believes in Mindsharing. Many other organizations and government agencies such as Procter & Gamble, Boeing, and NASA are tapping into the collective brainpower and creativity of a big crowd and utilizing the crowd to problem solve better, faster, and at less cost than ever imagined.

NASA, for example, has its own dedicated site or "pavilion" within InnoCentive and is challenging the crowd to solve problems ranging from how to keep food fresh in space, to forecasting solar events, and even how to develop a simple way for astronauts to do laundry during long-distance space travel or on the International Space Station. For that particular problem, NASA received almost 600 ideas from InnoCentive's pool of 300,000 "solvers."

Even intelligence agencies are using Mindsharing to improve their "intelligence forecasting," or ability to predict future critical events and create a better world. It's no secret that intelligence agencies are often criticized for not being able to predict and circumvent major events, from terrorist strikes to civil uprisings to whether a country does or does not have weapons of mass destruction. IARPA, or Intelligence Advanced Research Projects Activity (an offshoot of DARPA), is inviting the public to "try their hand at intelligence forecasting." It is sponsoring a few research projects in which crowds of nonexperts can go on missions and predict future critical events important to the intelligence community.

One of these research projects, which is managed at the University of Pennsylvania and at the University of California at Berkeley, is called the Good Judgment Project (www.good judgmentproject.com). The project began in 2011, and since then thousands of ordinary people have made their predictions on questions such as "Will Iran and the United States agree on a nuclear program?" or "Will Hamas militants in the Gaza Strip fire rockets into Israel?" According to one report, "the predictions made by the Good Judgment Project are often better than intelligence analysts with access to classified information."[4]

The research team at the Good Judgment Project has found a way to increase the forecasting accuracy by tracking the success of each forecaster over time. They found that when they take the top 2 percent of all participants, their collective forecasting is constantly more accurate than all other prediction methods.[5] They call this group "Super-Forecasters." These super-forecasters' collective predictions are often better than those of the CIA. You might wonder who these people are. Do they have education or experience in making such predictions?

One of the super-forecasters is Elaine Rich. She's sixty years old and when talking about her side job predicting global events says, "I'm just a pharmacist. Nobody cares about me, nobody knows my name, I don't have a professional reputation at stake. And it's this anonymity which actually gives me freedom to make true forecasts."[6]

Elaine is making forecasts such as estimating refugee flow in Syria from her kitchen in Maryland. According to the study cited on NPR, Elaine and other super-forecasters are 30 percent better at predicting future world events than intelligence officers with access to actual classified information. That might be due to groupthink inside the CIA. Volunteers don't have a secret agenda or any career risk associated with their estimates.

The research team compares each forecaster's prediction with what actually happens in the following months and years. For each question where a super-forecaster enters a probability greater than 50 percent of the event happening, this is counted as a "vote" that the outcome will occur. A positive prediction is made when the majority of super-forecasters make a positive vote for a specific outcome.

There's an ancient Jewish saying that prophecy is given to the fools. Don't get me wrong. I don't think that there's a single person capable of predicting the future. But many businesses depend on making accurate forecasts and predictions. It is such predictions that can make a business grow or disappear. If Kodak management could have gotten a better sense or prediction about the future of digital photography, they might have been saved from bankruptcy.

Business can learn from IARPA. If your business depends on making better forecasts, you might want to consider Mindsharing. But instead of using the collective intelligence of a big crowd, it's better if you pick the top 2 percent of performers from the crowd, and then take their collective prediction as strategic advice for your business.

There haven't been any longitudinal studies published at the time of writing this book to see if the crowd can make better predictions than those who are trained and educated to formulate geopolitical scenarios. Crowd wisdom tells us that a diverse enough crowd should give us equivalent intelligence. Unfortunately, the intelligence community is not openly sharing what they do, or who is responsible for either an accurate or inaccurate prediction of a political or global event. Dr. Dirk Warnaar, principal investigator for IARPA's forecasting project, has said that experts are often "so close to the subject matter at hand that they can form biases and may not be good forecasters."[7] Only the intelligence community itself will know if this particular way of Mindsharing is proven to be more accurate than the cloak-and-dagger, top-secret ways of the past, but unfortunately, I doubt they will ever tell.

If Mindsharing can help NASA solve complex issues involving microgravity, and help the CIA predict global events, it can certainly help you create a better résumé, gain valuable job experience, or even explore a new profession altogether. If you'd like to see a short video demo of the different Mindsharing resources that can help you manage your career, I've prepared such a video at this link: mindsharing.info/career.

FINDING YOUR PASSION

Hadas Vardi was a twenty-eight-year-old woman from Tel Aviv. She had worked in television programming for almost four years. She loved the television industry but not the temporary nature of her work and the unpredictability of television production and scheduling. Even though she loved her job, Hadas decided she needed to change professions. She had bills to pay. She was fast approaching thirty and it was time to make stability a priority over passion.

Hadas wanted to explore other directions for her professional life, but felt clueless about where to begin and what might be interesting for her to pursue. A few friends advised her to seek help from a professional career counselor who could expertly evaluate her skills and recommend new professions relevant to her talents.

After a few confusing months, Hadas had a different idea. She decided to post a Facebook status:

> I've decided to leave my career in the television industry. I'm looking for a new direction and stability, but I don't know what that is. This is why I've decided to have my own career day and I need your help. If you think your profession is interesting, fun, and allows you to earn a good living, maybe you'll agree to let me join you for one day at work. During this Take a Facebook Friend to Work Day, I'll be able to experience what you do and see if it fits my talent and passion.

Hadas received about fifty comments and many offers to join people at work, but more than that, countless people shared her status and complimented her for her courage and creativity. She screened all the offers she received and finally chose five people to join at work for a day.

At first, she was nervous about how welcome she would be at each workplace. She had never met some of these people and didn't know what to expect from spending a day with them at work. To her surprise, she was warmly welcomed at each workplace she visited. The employees were very helpful. She was able to experience the daily routines and have conversations with other employees and even a few CEOs. She learned what life is like when you are part of a start-up company. She spent a day at a small business that produces weddings. She learned the demands of being a photographer and running a photography business.

During each "career day," Hadas imagined what her life would be like if this were her job. And she waited and watched to see if she felt the same spark she felt going to work in the television industry every day. These were stable jobs. Stable professions. Hadas knew she wanted stability, but at the end of each day in the life of someone else, she still felt something was missing. She still felt lost and confused.

In the end, Hadas realized that more than stability, she wanted to go to work every day and do something she loved—something she was passionate about. She decided that she should stick with what she did best, the one thing that didn't feel like going to work at all—being a part of the television industry.

Mindsharing didn't help Hadas choose a new profession—it helped her choose her profession all over again. She was confident that although they had shortcomings, television programming and production were her true passions. It was a different kind of stability from the kind that ensured she could pay her bills every month, but Hadas relished the stability that came from being sure this was what she was meant to do with her life. The rest, she figured, would work itself out.

Hadas had hoped that through Mindsharing she would make a better decision about her career, and no one was more surprised than Hadas to find that Mindsharing led her to exactly the place best suited for her—right where she was. We can't always predict where Mindsharing will lead us when it comes to our careers or our life, but we can be assured it is most often the exact place we need to be.

3.

LINKING IN AND LINKING OUT
(Mindsharing on LinkedIn)

In the two seconds it takes you to read this sentence, four new people will have joined LinkedIn. With more than 260 million members, there is no doubt that LinkedIn is the best site for Mindsharing among experts. When it comes to searching for a job, building business connections, and career recruiting, LinkedIn is the place to go on the Web.

I consider myself quite well informed and knowledgeable about the ins and outs (so to speak) of LinkedIn. If you are not so familiar with LinkedIn, an Amazon search would reveal 2,145 books about the subject, and who has time to read 2,145 books? I decided to do a Mindsharing experiment with my Facebook crowd. I posted this as my status:

> I'm using LinkedIn to build a network of professional connections, but I wonder what is the real value of LinkedIn. I go there every few months to approve new connections and that's it. From your experience, what is the most important thing to do there? Thanks.

After getting almost a hundred comments in response to my post, I met with a leading LinkedIn expert and shared with him the insights I gained from the crowd. It was time to test the basic premise of Mindsharing, that a big, diverse crowd will give you an answer as good as any expert's.

My crowd came up with the main things you need to do to maximize the potential of LinkedIn to enhance your career. I am happy to say these were the main points the LinkedIn expert had as well.

If you already know everything you need to know about LinkedIn (or have read the 2,145 books), please feel free to skip ahead in the chapter to the discussion on Mindsharing within LinkedIn; otherwise we will go over the key things you need to do in LinkedIn before you begin Mindsharing.

LINKEDIN ESSENTIALS

The number one piece of advice from my crowd and from the LinkedIn expert was that your LinkedIn profile is everything. It is your online résumé, and the professional face you present to the world. It is important that your professional face boasts a professional picture. Unlike Facebook where you might share that crazy picture of you doing a keg-stand from your college days, LinkedIn is the place where people will check you out if they want to do business with you or hire you. Nobody wants to do business with a guy based on his ability to do a handstand on a keg while drinking beer upside down. Your LinkedIn profile is seven times more likely to be viewed if you have a profile picture. That blue faceless silhouette may be the easiest route to go on your profile, but it won't get the results you are looking for. Nobody wants to do business with a silhouette. Choose your photo wisely.

Next in your profile will be your work experience, your education, and your areas of expertise and skill. Be detailed and thorough here. There is also a section where you can summarize who you are as a professional. LinkedIn suggests your summary should be a minimum of forty words in order to increase your odds of appearing in someone's search. Looking for a job? You can use the search option under the jobs menu, and don't forget to use glassdoor.com (mentioned in the previous chapter) to get inside information about employment opportunities. When creating your summary, make sure it includes specific keywords that relate to that job description. This isn't the place to be overly creative in your wordsmithing. In fact, describing yourself as a wordsmith (although poetic) is less likely to get you searched and found than simply describing yourself as a skilled writer. There are common words and phrases used in job descriptions for any field—find the ones used in your field and incorporate them within your summary. Also avoid superlatives in your summary or résumé. Some recruiters and employers will automatically filter these out. Sure, you may in fact be "super smart" or "wildly team oriented," but this is not the place to word it this way.

Make it a habit to log in to your profile often in order to approve new connection requests and check your inbox. You never know when a new and exciting opportunity will come your way through one of your network connections. LinkedIn suggests updating your profile once a month so you are always current with your accomplishments and milestones. Think about any interesting projects you have been a part of. Don't be shy about your expertise. Let the professional world know who you are. Whether you are looking for a job, or wanting to move up within your organization, keeping an updated LinkedIn profile will help you reach the next stage in your career. Potential business partners and recruiters will seek you out, and more often than not, LinkedIn is what will provide them with their first impression of you. Think of your profile as the first handshake—make it firm, solid, and a bold statement of who you are professionally. Nobody likes a limp or weak handshake. The same goes for a limp or weak LinkedIn profile.

If you haven't been on LinkedIn in a while you will see many new features (which is yet another reason to log in and update your profile often). There is an often-overlooked section for "Volunteering & Causes." Do you work at a local homeless shelter? Do you fund-raise for a particular cause near and dear to your heart? List them on your LinkedIn profile. According to LinkedIn research, 42 percent of hiring managers surveyed say they view volunteer experience as equal to work experience.[1]

Endorsements are another feature in LinkedIn. Endorsements let your connections vote on the skills and areas of expertise you've listed for yourself. They also have the ability to recommend new skills that you may not have previously listed in your profile. This is where it gets tricky, however. Endorsement bombing is where members will endorse connections for random and often absurd skills such as "use of the f-bomb," "kidnapping and ransom," or "roundhouse kicks." Now you may deliver a mean roundhouse kick while dropping an "f-bomb" in a kidnap and ransom attempt, but this is probably not the skill set you want to be most voted on in your profile for potential new business ventures. The good news is that you can edit your endorsements, remove some, or choose not to display endorsements at all.

The final profile feature worth noting is the ability to add rich media to your profile. You can add video, photos, documents, and presentations that display your skills, accomplishments, or projects. It's one thing to tell about your accomplishments in your profile, and another thing to show them in all their full-color glory.

Creating and maintaining your LinkedIn profile is critical. Update it often but be mindful that every time you update, your connections are notified (including your boss, if he's a connection). There is a way to hide your updates under settings, if this is an issue. View the profiles of people you admire in your field and note their keywords, their summary, and their endorsements.

Here is a sample LinkedIn profile that we can all measure our profiles against.

Summary

I'm the happiest guy you'll ever meet. My cheer is infectious, and I get thrills spreading it at scale. I love children too. I thrive on their faith in me. The combination of these two passions is why I'm in the business of making kids smile.

My idea of fun is patiently listening to whiny customers seated on my lap in a mall, and turning their toy requests into $500 billion in sales. I'm proud that I have a direct impact on their behavior too: Nice? Gifts. Naughty? Coal.

I can wear many hats: postal worker, reindeer tamer, workshop executive, sleigh pilot, chimney gymnast and elf resources manager. Desk jobs aren't for me though. I do my best work on the move, flying through the sky.

I manage a team of 300,000 three-foot direct reports who live and breathe generosity and goodness. I know how to get the most out of them too. Since the launch of my elf-training program, my letter-readers have cut time-per-letter by 39%, and my toy builders, wrappers and loaders have increased their output by 17%.

I can brave arctic temperatures and overcome sleep deprivation. I can shimmy up and down chimneys in a flash — without making a peep. No chimney? No problem. I'll figure out how to get in.

I'm the kind of guy who is so meticulous that when I make my list in Excel, I check it twice. I have an uncanny ability to know when my customers are sleeping, and when they're awake.

Despite the demands of the job, I've never missed my annual deadline. Ever. Some people don't even believe in me, yet I still deliver to them–on time.

Skills & Expertise

Most endorsed for...

27	Manufacturing Operations Management
13	Postal Optimization
12	Employee Training
12	Product Development
11	Leadership
9	Animal Welfare
9	Business Travel
6	Manual Labor

Once your profile is fine-tuned, the next essential step is simple—grow your digital network. LinkedIn allows you to import your e-mail contacts from multiple sources (Gmail, Yahoo, and many others) and send out an invitation to your list to connect to your network via LinkedIn. This is an extremely effective, one-time activity to grow your initial network. After that, whenever you meet someone or read about someone you find interesting, you can send them a LinkedIn invitation. It's far more effective than asking someone for their business card. People change employers, people change positions, and while business cards can become dated, you'll always be able to get in touch with someone through LinkedIn and also be able to follow their career progression.

The last essential area to cover for LinkedIn is a little feature called "Send InMail." Say you want to e-mail Arianna Huffington, Bill Gates, Richard Branson, or some other high-ranking executive who works for a company you are interested in doing business with. It's not always easy to get Bill Gates's e-mail address—even for someone who used to work at Microsoft.

However, if they are on LinkedIn, and most executives are among the 260 million who are, you can send an e-mail directly to them using the internal e-mail feature of LinkedIn. It's not a free feature, but if your career can benefit from being able to directly e-mail the CEO of a local tech company you'd like to work for, I highly recommend getting a subscription to LinkedIn Premium. With it you have direct access to almost anyone, even me.

MINDSHARING AMONG EXPERTS

There are hundreds of thousands of LinkedIn Groups. Each group's members have the same professional areas of interest.

For example, there are groups for product managers, physicians, lawyers, and almost any other profession you can imagine. These groups are where Mindsharing on LinkedIn takes place.

After joining a group, you can ask questions and get answers from experts in your field of interest. Search for the largest groups that best describe your profession. For example, if you are a marketing professional you would perhaps search under marketing (or advertising, communication, etc.). Now this search will give you more than fifty-two thousand results in groups, but you can narrow it down by size and relevance. If you see a group that looks promising you can click on the name and then the information icon to see the group's profile and statistics. This will tell you how many members are in the group, how active the group is, and also the demographics of the group and the percentage of members who are senior level in their field.

After joining a group, look at the discussion page and see what kinds of questions members are asking. Some groups have rules, so make sure you view any rules that apply to the group you've joined. Then give it a try—ask your own question. Mindsharing on LinkedIn is a powerful tool that can save you time and money, and potentially solve your most difficult career or business questions.

(For a readymade list of the best LinkedIn groups for Mindsharing, organized by profession, please go to mindsharing.info /linkedin.)

Sai Krusshna is a twenty-four-year-old student from Malaysia. Before he began studying for his master's degree in information technology management at Staffordshire University, Sai was the operations supervisor and partner at a dairy farm in India. Sai was responsible for managing many projects on the dairy farm, some of which failed. When it was time to do his master's thesis, Sai recalled many frustrating days on the dairy farm, and decided to explore why projects fail.

Sai spent almost a hundred hours trying to figure out why physical projects fail. He read countless articles, research papers, and books—some of which were valuable, but many were a waste of his time. At the end of his grueling hundred hours of study, Sai still didn't have what he needed to develop his thesis on why projects fail.

Frustrated, Sai decided to try something else—Mindsharing on LinkedIn. He logged in to LinkedIn and found a group called "The Project Manager Network—#1 Group for Project Managers." This group had 487,163 members, all experienced project managers. After joining, Sai posed his question to the group:

> Hi, I'm a master's student. I'm planning to do my thesis on why projects fail. Any suggestions on which aspects I should focus on in particular?

Sai waited to get a response from this group. He received 269 responses from project managers around the world. After spending weeks exploring his thesis subject, Sai Mindshared with a crowd of experts and found the answers he was looking for in just one hour. The crowd gave Sai a clear sense of where he should focus his research—communication among teams— and convinced him to narrow the scope of his work.

Sai found a valuable resource in this one LinkedIn group, and his insights about why projects fail helped not only him but countless other members of this group who learned from his Mindsharing challenge. As we see time and again when we Mindshare, value is contagious, and a problem shared is a problem solved.

STREAMLINE YOUR WORK

Mindsharing on LinkedIn can help your business in other ways as well. Tamir Huberman is a senior vice president at a technology transfer company in Israel. His organization takes academic patents and licenses them to commercial organizations interested in implementing the patent. One of the patents Tamir needed to sell was a patent that could transform an airplane seat into a "smart chair." When he told me about it, I immediately smiled. I love how everything around us has become "smart." I can have a smart television, a smart watch, and even smart glasses. Smart chairs on an airplane? What a great idea. Would it book my travel for me? Sing me to sleep on a long flight? Check my e-mail for me?

Then Tamir brought me back from my daydreams about "smart" furniture and explained that it wasn't what I was imagining—it was a chair that could significantly reduce deep vein thrombosis (DVT), a potentially fatal condition also known as "economy class syndrome." It is believed to affect millions of air passengers a year. DVT is caused by prolonged, immobile sitting within a limited space and with insufficient legroom. Economy class.

In the past, in order to do his job, Tamir would have to invest up to a year researching organizations and people within those organizations who might be interested in a particular patent. Once he found the organizations and the contact people within those organizations, he would then need to find a way to get in direct contact with those executives. Not always easy, as we've discussed.

That was his past methodology, but Tamir has discovered Mindsharing within LinkedIn and found a way to streamline this year-long process. Armed with his airplane smart-chair patent, Tamir posted information about DVT and simply asked, "Who do you think might be interested in this patent?" in a few relevant LinkedIn groups, and after twenty-four hours he had a complete list of relevant organizations and contact people. Mindsharing on LinkedIn turned one year of work into one day of work. Tamir couldn't have been happier. More than that, someone from a group told him about an upcoming conference solely dedicated to airline seat manufacturers (apparently there is a conference for everything). Through Mindsharing on LinkedIn, Tamir was able to completely map the market and contact the key people he needed to sell this patent. In the future, if you are sitting still for too long in your airplane seat and are at risk for DVT, the built-in seat sensors may just alert the crew, and you will have Tamir and Mindsharing to thank for saving you from a great big pain in your . . .

MINDSHARING AND THE CHIEF LISTENING OFFICER

In the age of CEO, COO, CFO, and other three-letter acronyms that signal that a position is important inside an organization, there is a rising need to create a CLO (Chief Listening Officer). Whether it's on LinkedIn or Twitter or Facebook, your customers and your employees are talking about your company, your product, and your work culture. The CLO is responsible for listening to what is being said, and is the likely person to be in charge of Mindsharing within your organization. Listening is time-consuming, but not listening can be costly.

All Mindsharing requires mastering the art of listening. Some businesses do it well, some don't do it well. And customers are savvy about the difference. Pepperidge Farm is a company that does it well. In 2013 an obscure blogger wrote a piece called "The Milano: An Ode to Pepperidge Farm."[2] In his blog, he wrote about his newfound love for the Milano cookie. Pepperidge Farm, which must have had a CLO actively listening for mention of the company (thank you, Google Alerts), read the post and not only listened, but responded. The blogger, Rob Gunther, received a personal note from Pepperidge Farm along with a very large supply of Milano cookies.

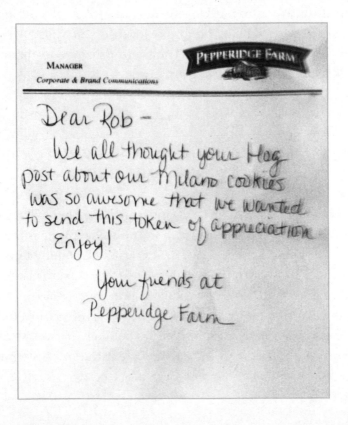

This is an example of a company that's listening correctly. They not only won a customer forever, but as Rob shared his surprise with his crowd, the company received media interest and PR worth far more than the cost of two dozen bags of cookies.

Not every company or business, however, has mastered the art of listening and responding correctly. When a customer posted to the Facebook page of Domino's pizza raving about her order, someone wasn't listening and Domino's responded with an automatic apology rather than a thank-you.

A CLO is about much more than providing great customer service or doing PR work. When organizations *really* listen to customers and actively Mindshare, they will respond by either changing or modifying their business practices, developing new products, or targeting their marketing and advertising efforts differently. Crowd wisdom can help focus a business plan, direct future strategies, provide better services to its customers, and create future brand or company loyalty. Mindsharing with your customers, showing that you value the wisdom they offer, creates customers who are invested in the success of your business. It creates personal connections that are invaluable.

When I worked at Microsoft, I was involved in the launch of Windows Vista. That launch failed miserably, and suffice it to say that if you are on a PC, you are most likely not using Windows Vista. Today, in the age of social media, mistakes such as this one would never happen because Windows Vista would never have been launched with its various bugs, incompatibility issues, and slow performance. If customers who are beta testing a product today say it's not ready, companies (that are listening) will not release that product. If they ignore the wisdom of the crowd, the crowd can kill a product before it even gets to market.

People want to feel heard and listened to, and this is as true in business as it is in our personal life. Pay attention to what your customers and employees are saying online, and learn from and adapt to the wisdom of the crowd.

A CAUTIONARY TALE

As we enter the digital age, the demarcation between our business life and our personal life can get quite blurry. In December 2013, a New York PR executive posted a tweet as she was boarding a flight from London to go on holiday in South Africa. It was her personal account, and the tweet (about Africa and AIDS) was meant to be funny but came across the Twittersphere as racist and insensitive. By the time she had landed in South Africa, her tweet was known as "The Tweet Heard 'Round the World," the hashtag #hasjustinelandedyet had gone viral, someone had registered a domain name with her name and directed it to a donation page for AIDS relief in Africa, and she had been fired from her company. In the course of one short flight and because of one insensitive tweet, this PR executive was not only out of a job, but most likely out of any future career in public relations.

Companies are listening online. They are listening to their customers, and they are listening to their employees. And if you are looking for a job, trust and believe that your social media presence, your LinkedIn profile, and your tweets will all be vetted. You can change your privacy settings on Facebook so that you control who sees your posts, your photos, and your activities, but Twitter is in the public domain, and as the PR executive from New York learned, your entire career can be changed in 140 characters or less.

Mindsharing is a great tool for your career and business, but the medium in which it operates has hazards that can affect both your career and (as we will explore in Part Three) your personal life. In business, we are more connected than ever, and while this offers great potential for your professional life, it also comes with pitfalls. As you manage your LinkedIn profile, your Twitter accounts, and your Facebook page, ask yourself if there's anything you wouldn't want your boss to see. Your customers to see. Your colleagues to see. And make your choices accordingly. Social media is still a relatively new landscape for businesses, and in the next chapter we will explore how to manage digital relationships so that your Mindsharing is both purposeful and effective.

PART 2

THE ART OF MINDSHARING

4.

WORKING THE CROWD
(Managing Digital Relationships)

We have explored how and where to build your crowd, and I've walked you through some of the amazing ways Mindsharing can help your career. This chapter is all about building and managing relationships online. Real relationships take time and effort to maintain, and so does the relationship you have with your crowd. Like all relationships, there needs to be balance. If you are spending all your time Mindsharing ways to be a better parent, but forget to actually spend time with your children, this is not balance.

A few years ago, while having breakfast in a neighborhood café, I watched two young girls greet each other as they waited in line to get ice cream. They were happy to see each other, and I heard one tell the other that she had something very important to tell her. "But not here," she added. "Let's talk tonight on Facebook."

I was surprised at the exchange. I wanted to get up and tell the first girl: "You are friends, aren't you? You have something very important to tell your friend, don't you? You are just waiting in line to get some ice cream. So why don't you say what you have to say right now?"

In Israel, it is quite common for people to give their opinion to perfect strangers, but I held my tongue.

It took me some time to understand what had happened in the café, and why it was so puzzling to me. The unspoken understanding between these two friends was that they could have a better, and more private, conversation digitally than they could face-to-face in an ice cream shop (where strangers would be waiting to jump in and offer their opinions).

Managing relationships in the digital world is not second nature to those of us who were born before the Internet. But for young people, digital natives, it's very natural. They inherently know that every communication method has its advantages and disadvantages. They navigate the digital world of relationships with ease and comfort.

Some of us need a little more help.

HEALTHY RELATIONSHIPS 101

In order to Mindshare effectively, we must have a healthy digital relationship with our crowd. This means that we must learn how to manage our time, information, numbers, people, places, and conversations digitally.

If you are Mindsharing within one of the external platforms— Quora, LinkedIn groups—you don't need to spend a whole lot of time and effort managing your relationship with the crowd. You can post your Mindsharing question (hopefully it is a good and effective question, which we will discuss in the next chapter) and wait for the results. If it is an internal crowd—Facebook or Twitter—then you need to manage your relationship with the crowd in the same ways you would manage any important relationship in your life.

Gary Vaynerchuk is one of the great thought leaders in the world of social media. With more than a million followers on Twitter, he is an expert at using digital tools in order to build a community. Gary regularly publishes a video blog, and he is an expert at engaging his crowd and reaching out to his fans.

I asked Gary directly what he thought to be the single most important element in building digital relationships. His answer was simple—effort. You get out what you put in, and this is true whether you are in a relationship with one or one million.

NO ONE-NIGHT STANDS

When you build your crowd for Mindsharing, remember you are in it for the long haul. You are looking for a long-term relationship, not a one-night stand. Build the relationship accordingly. Don't rush things. Don't be pushy or grabby. In other words—don't immediately go for a Mindsharing home run without first touching all the bases. You need to get to know your crowd and your crowd needs to get to know you. This is how trust and intimacy are built. If you are looking for a Mindsharing relationship without commitment, then limit your Mindsharing to large, external platforms, where you can engage with a big crowd that doesn't have to know who you are. You won't even have to give your real name. Ask your question, get your answers, and get out. This is the "hit it and quit it" version of Mindsharing. It may not be the most fulfilling of relationships, but it gets the job done.

When you are building an internal network, it takes time, effort, and patience. You won't have ten thousand followers overnight who are ready and willing to solve every life decision with you. But if you engage the crowd, "date" the crowd, and treat the crowd with respect—in the end you will have a mutually satisfying relationship that will lead to a lifetime of successful Mindsharing. It could take a few months, or even a year, before you and your crowd are "mutually committed." Perhaps you already have a large crowd and are ready to take things to the next level in your relationship. The dos and don'ts of managing digital relationships are the same whether you are building your crowd one by one, or already have a willing and able crowd in place.

IS ANYBODY OUT THERE?

When I first started writing my blog, I felt a profound sense of loneliness. Was anyone out there? Was anyone reading what I wrote? Was it even worth the time and effort? I wanted the love of a big crowd, but I wasn't sure how to go about getting it. I made the decision to be authentic and to never compromise my values in exchange for a larger audience. I wrote only about things I was genuinely passionate about and inspired by— technology, innovation in marketing through social media, cool gadgets that made my life easier, and personal stories about my daughter and how she was growing up a digital native in the digital age. I also shared my enthusiasm about the medium I was working with—blogging. It was a relatively new concept at the time, and I saw a huge potential for connection and value. My most popular posts were those where I shared stories about interesting events and happenings in my life, and also where I shared personal stories about my daughter and family. I learned that storytelling is just as valuable and important in the digital world as it is in our daily face-to-face interactions.

My least popular posts were those where I didn't have an interesting story to share or when I failed to share something meaningful to me. And meaningful doesn't have to imply something deeply profound or wise. It just has to be real. You can post a funny cat video because you know cat videos are popular and they might increase your audience response. Or you can post a video of your own cat, and share the story of how you came to own her, or what this cat means in your life. Both videos may be funny, but one will be real.

Mindsharing demands an uncompromising commitment to what is real because the crowd can always spot a hidden agenda. I didn't have a big audience at first, but I chose not to compromise, to be persistent, and over time, my small crowd began to grow. People began to find value in my blog and began to share it with their friends. Value, of course, is a subjective concept. As you define value for yourself and for your crowd, it is good to ask yourself these questions: What is it that makes me think? What makes me curious? What makes me feel inspired? What brings humor to my life? What makes me consider others? What makes me happy, or a better person today than the person I was yesterday? Within the answers, you will find your value.

Here's a small experiment you can try. Watch your Facebook news feed for fifteen or twenty minutes, and read each status update from your friends. For each one, ask yourself—does it give me value? Now, when I do this exercise (and let me say that I love my Facebook friends and consider them valuable), for the most part, the content I see does not contain a lot of value. Status updates such as *I just woke up*, or *I don't feel good*, or *Having a great day*, don't really add value to my life. Many people tend to share things they are doing or things that happen to them, and while nice (sometimes), it's better to share something that will be valuable to your crowd.

The big question is, if the fact that you are watching your carbs is not going to give value to your crowd—what is it that gives value? Perhaps your passion is food and cooking. Maybe you dream of being a chef one day and having your own cooking show. If so, sharing your excitement and passion about cooking is what will give value to your crowd. Share with them something amazing you have learned about food.

Don't share what you ate for dinner.

Do share links to recipes, stories about your cooking adventures, YouTube videos with inspiring chefs, or funny things that happened to you as you were learning to cook. This will give value. This will engage your crowd. This will help them see the bigger story about what you are sharing.

Here's a practical example. You dream of being a talented chef. You want to engage with your crowd and give value. You've just hosted a dinner party and received many compliments on your excellent apple pie.

Here are five possible posts you could make, from low to high value:

1. "I made a great apple pie."

2. "Here's a picture of the apple pie I baked tonight. My friends said it was amazing!"

3. "The secret to making a great apple pie is [XYZ]."

4. "I just had friends for dinner. I made this apple pie, which was devoured in two minutes [picture]. Here's my recipe. The secret to a great apple pie is [XYZ]."

5. "I just had friends for dinner. I made this apple pie, which was devoured in two minutes. Here's a link to my blog with the recipe and a video showing you how to make it. Give it a try and let me know how it goes!"

As you can see, the first example simply shares a fact about something that happened. It has no inherent value for the crowd. There is nothing in the post that will make people care. Nothing for them to learn. No reason for them to share it or engage.

If you look at the last post, there is the potential for great value. This isn't to say everyone in your crowd is now going to bake an apple pie. But they may want to learn your secret. They may share it with their relative who loves to bake. They may get involved with your story and passion for being a chef because they've now visited your blog.

This is just one example, but it holds true for anything you are passionate about—law, tax reform, health care, the sexual habits of mollusks—anything. The secret ingredient for managing digital relationships (not baking pies) is repeatedly giving value—day after day, post after post. People who share your passions and interests will join in.

This is what makes Mindsharing possible.

THANK YOU VERY MUCH

Once you put in the effort, give value, and engage your crowd in Mindsharing, you must show appreciation. All relationships thrive when partners appreciate the contributions of one another. A little thank-you goes a long way.

When I came back from giving my TED talk, I wanted to

thank all those who helped me create my talk and make my dream come true. I invited my crowd to a "thank-you" meeting that I held at the university where I teach. I tried to thank each person specifically for their contribution and show how much *I* valued *their* value.

The biggest contributor to my successful TED appearance was Or Sagy, the sixteen-year-old boy who came up with the idea for me to bring a real ox onto the TED stage. While I was in Long Beach (not far from Hollywood) I bought a replica of an Academy Award statue. During my group thank-you, I called Or up onto the stage and presented him with his Academy Award. The audience gave him a standing ovation. It was a beautiful moment, and my crowd felt how much I appreciated them for their Mindsharing contributions.

Now, every time you get brilliant Mindsharing ideas or solutions from your crowd you don't need to rent out a large venue and present them with awards—but you do need to show your appreciation. Say thank you. Acknowledge that you are aware your crowd is taking time away from the concerns of their own lives to help you out. When you have a big crowd, you will not be able to thank and communicate with each and every person, but when you appreciate the work of those who engage with you, everyone in the crowd sees this and knows that you are giving back. No one wants to be in a relationship with someone who takes more than they give. Appreciate your crowd. Do it soon and do it often. Thank them for their opinions, their ideas, their time, and their efforts.

WE ALL MAKE MISTAKES

If you are new to growing a crowd, managing a crowd, and Mindsharing, you will make mistakes. None of us is born knowing how to perfectly manage our relationships, but often we learn best from the mistakes we make.

Unlike the real world, however, the digital world has a quick and easy way to end a relationship—the "unfriend" button. If I don't like something my cousin or aunt or uncle says to me on vacation, I can't simply unfriend them and go about my life. If my best friend disagrees with me, I can't simply "block" him and pretend he never existed.

But at any moment, any member of your crowd is just a click away from disappearing forever. You don't want that to happen.

Let's review the most common mistakes, and the quickest way to sabotage your Mindsharing success:

1. SELLING. If you are always trying to sell your crowd something, they will quickly disappear. People have NO SOLICITING signs on their doors for a reason. No one likes to feel like they are constantly being pitched a product or bombarded with advertising. The quickest way to make your crowd disengage or even unfriend you is to make them feel you are pushing a hidden agenda.

2. NOT ENGAGING. Your crowd will soon lose interest if you don't quickly respond to them or acknowledge their contributions. If you are asked a question, answer it. Mindsharing is a reciprocal relationship. If you don't make the effort, as we discussed previously, or you don't show appreciation, your

crowd will get bored (at the very least) and move elsewhere or simply stop responding. No one likes to feel used.

3. DISAPPEARING. Imagine you are in a long-term relationship, and your partner suddenly disappears. No phone calls. No text messages. Nothing but radio silence. How would you feel? I imagine you wouldn't feel very good about it. The same goes for your crowd. It's easy to dip in and out of the digital world, sometimes too easy. If you are going on a silent retreat for ten days, going offline for a month, traveling on a remote tropical island where Wi-Fi doesn't exist—whatever it is, let your crowd know you will be offline for a while. Don't just disappear, or you may come back to find your crowd has also disappeared.

4. OFFENDING. Don't forget your values. If you live them in real life, live them in your digital life. Just because your crowd isn't in front of you doesn't mean you have license to say anything offensive or insulting from behind the safety of your computer screen. Respect your crowd and they will respect you back. If you do offend (and it happens), apologize immediately. Everyone makes mistakes, and everyone has the power to own up to it, apologize, and ensure it never happens again. This is what I had to do when I infiltrated a women-only group on Facebook. I took my lumps and learned from my mistake.

CAN I BORROW YOUR WIFE?

Imagine someone walking up to you and saying, "Hey, I really like your wife. She seems pretty powerful. She really gets the job done, and I see you are having great success with her. Can I borrow her for this one thing I'm trying out?" A person wanting to use your crowd is the same idea.

After I began mastering the art of Mindsharing, many friends and colleagues wanted me to demonstrate the power of Mindsharing. They wanted me to ask my crowd questions on their behalf. At first, I was so infatuated with the success of Mindsharing and so excited about sharing it with others that I Mindshared for myself, I Mindshared for my friends, I passed my crowd around like it was a cheap toy from the dollar store.

My crowd did not like this.

Not one bit.

My Facebook friends began complaining that I was bothering them. I was asking too many questions, and they could tell some of the questions were not mine. They felt used.

I felt ashamed.

I immediately stopped my loose behavior with the crowd. Now whenever someone comes and asks to "use" my crowd, I say a polite but firm no. I treat my crowd as I would treat anyone in my life whose relationship I value. I cherish it. I nurture it. I make sure I never take more than I give. And I refuse to do anything that will cheapen our relationship. I don't waste my crowd's time.

Respect is a two-way street, in real-world relationships and in digital relationships. If you treat your crowd as you would treat any relationship you value, it will be there for you when you need it. If not, you will find your crowd dwindling before your eyes.

5.

MIRROR, MIRROR, ON THE WALL
(Asking the Right Questions)

> Judge a man by his questions rather than by his answers.
>
> **VOLTAIRE**

The average preschooler asks his or her parents anywhere between one hundred and three hundred questions per day.[1] *Why is the sky blue? Why does my nose stick out of my face? Where do babies come from?* The average teenager likely asks his or her parents zero questions (except for the occasional *Can I have some money? Can I borrow the car?*). What about you? When was the last time you went to work and asked your coworker or boss a multitude of questions? What would the reaction have been? Somewhere along the way to being grown-ups, we stop asking questions. Perhaps we learn at some point in school, or in our jobs, that we are rewarded and valued for having the answers, not for asking the questions.

To utilize the power of Mindsharing, you have to be willing to ask questions—a lot of questions. Not a hundred or more questions a day like a preschooler, but enough questions so that you can tap into the collective intelligence and wisdom that resides within the crowd. Some questions will lead to intelligence and wisdom, and some will not. There is an art to asking questions, and in this chapter we will explore what types of questions lead to effective Mindsharing, and what types of

questions will lead your crowd to respond to you like a tired
parent who has just been asked for the thousandth time, *Why is
water wet?*

SO MANY QUESTIONS—SO LITTLE TIME

I know what constitutes an effective question in Mindsharing,
because I have written many ineffective questions. To be effective, a Mindsharing question must be clear, detailed, and specific. Ideally it should tell a story and also be meaningful in
some way.

Imagine you are at a dinner party. Someone you don't know
very well comes up to you and engages you in conversation.
They are a friend of a friend—more an acquaintance than anything. The conversation is awkward, the questions a bit stilted.
*What about this weather? How about those Mets? So what do you do for
a living? How do you know the host?* We all know the sort of idle
chitchat and superficial questions that inform conversations
like these. There is no real depth, no real connection, and no
true relationship that comes from these sorts of questions.
When you Mindshare with your crowd, you don't want your
questions to be the equivalent of mindless dinner party small
talk. If the question is not important, or if its answer can easily
be found in a Google search, don't ask it. No one has time for
idle questions. No one wants to engage if the conversation is
not meaningful. You don't want to be the guest that people try
to avoid at the dinner party.

A good question tells a story to show there is context and a
good reason for asking the question in the first place. It's authentic. It's a subtle difference, but we all know the difference

between an authentic question and an inauthentic question. It's the difference between your best friend asking, "How are you?" and the teller at the bank asking, "How are you?" There's a different quality to the question and a different invitation to answer. Questions are always invitations, and when we invite the crowd to Mindshare we must do it from a place of humility and with honesty.

BE SPECIFIC

Before you ask the crowd a question, ask yourself this: "What is it that I am specifically asking the crowd to do?" When I was buying a car after leaving Microsoft I was very specific about my needs. I didn't ask a general question such as, "I'm looking for

a new car. What do you recommend?" Or, "I need new transportation. What should I get?" If I had asked the question this way, I would have most likely received all sorts of answers that weren't suitable to the needs of my family. Yes, I'd like to drive the Batmobile or an amphibious combat vehicle, but neither will probably have the attachments I need to lock down the baby's car seat.

I received more than a hundred responses to my detailed and specific question about what kind of car I should buy to meet the needs of my family. I didn't have to weed through dozens of crazy answers from the crowd, because I was clear in what I was asking. Also, my crowd didn't have to engage in a lot of back-and-forth questions getting clarification. If your questions are not specific and well defined, you won't get the amazing benefits that are the hallmark of Mindsharing—saved time, saved money, and knowledge equal to that of an expert.

BE BRIEF

People have lives to live and decisions to make that are just as important as yours. If you are asking people to take the time to Mindshare with you, respect their time. Be direct. Get to the point. State your question clearly. And then step back and let the Mindsharing magic go to work. Tell people only what they need to know to answer the question. If they have more questions, they will ask you. Don't waste your time and don't waste the time of your crowd.

If you are Mindsharing on Twitter, you have to ask your questions in 140 characters or less, so brevity isn't really an issue. On Facebook, however, you can go on (and on) for almost as long as you like. And some people do overly indulge. Facebook's character limit is now 63,206. That's a little less than the length of this chapter to this point. (If you're curious, the Facebook world record for the longest status update is 62,896 characters.) No one has time to read seven or eight pages of text in a status update, and people rarely look forward to clicking the "See More" link in a status update.

There are exceptions to this rule, however, and times when you need to tell a story to give context and relevance to your question. We are storytellers by nature, and there are instances where a story will inspire or motivate your crowd to Mindshare more than simply asking the question alone would. If you do need to tell a story first, remember to still make the question itself clear, specific, and brief.

When I was invited to give a talk at a biotech conference, I decided to Mindshare with my crowd for creative ideas for the conference. It was an important talk, but instead of just asking the question, I felt the need to share the story of how I came to give this talk. It was a conscious decision I made, and one I believed would result in a better quality of Mindsharing.

This was the story I posted to the crowd:

I received a phone call today that began like this:

"Hi Lior. This is Sharon speaking (not her real name). I have an offer for you, but before I give it to you, please take a deep breath."

Such calls make me nervous. I took a deep breath and listened attentively.

"In two weeks there's going to be a big international biotech conference. The opening keynote speaker was supposed to be Israeli president Shimon Peres. Unfortunately for him and for us, at the last minute he had to cancel because of an important diplomatic visit. We want to ask you to replace him at the opening keynote."

At this moment, my heart was beating twice as fast as normal. I mumbled, "Thank you, and I cannot believe you are saying my name and Shimon Peres's name in the same sentence. . . ."

I'm thrilled to have a chance to speak at this conference, and I'm preparing my keynote about Mindsharing and crowd wisdom as it relates to the medical world.

I'm looking for ideas for audience engagement. It could be something similar to what I did with the ox but related to the medical world. Something simple, it can also be a picture. It should be interesting and relevant.

Do you have any ideas? I promise to update you when I find a great idea from the crowd.

In this instance, I felt the need to tell the story of how I came to be looking for creative ideas from my crowd. Because the story was so meaningful for me, it engaged my crowd in a way that it might not have if I had just posed the question. I also promised them a reward. Not a monetary reward, but an implicit reward. I promised to update them. I promised to share the crowd-generated idea at a big conference. I promised them some value in return for their value. This is as important as thanking the crowd, as we mentioned in the previous chapter.

You must decide when a story will help the quality of wisdom you get from the crowd, or when a story will only hinder or distract the crowd.

I received many wonderful ideas from my crowd after sharing this story and asking for help. Ultimately, however, I had misguided my crowd. It turned out that the audience wouldn't comprise doctors but biotech industry professionals. I didn't end up doing a live experiment for this crowd, but it wasn't because I didn't get helpful ideas from the crowd. It was because I was not clear and specific enough with my crowd.

I still stood in for Shimon Peres, and it still makes my heart beat fast when I think of it.

DON'T DO THIS

Here are some of the top mistakes I've made in asking questions:

ASKING TOO MANY QUESTIONS. No one likes to be nagged. If you're bored at home and asking too many questions for the sake of asking questions (or you are new to Mindsharing and drunk on its power), your crowd will tune you out faster than you can say "Mindsharing." Mindsharing isn't about pressuring or nagging the crowd into doing your decision making for you (remember, it's about inviting your crowd). If you have a million Mindsharing questions that absolutely must be asked now, then spread them out over different platforms and spare your crowd the burden of your manic Mindsharing. The quality of results you get will be far greater if you do not treat your crowd as your own personal search engine.

NOT LISTENING. Mindsharing is a dialogue, not a monologue. Listen to the answers your crowd gives you, show appreciation for their ideas, ask questions, and engage with the crowd as much as they engage with you (or more). If someone comes up with a brilliant idea or answer to your question, acknowledge their brilliance. Let them know how much they've helped you. Mindsharing is not a solo activity—it's a relationship. (If you are confused by this, reread the previous chapter on managing digital relationships.)

GIVING CHOICES. Mindsharing is not a survey. It is a process of gathering crowd wisdom. Ask questions that are open ended, that don't have a yes or no answer or a choice between two options. Trust the crowd to think for itself—that's how you get collective intelligence and crowd wisdom.

LEADING. Do not lead the witness. This is a bit more subtle than asking a survey question, but along the same lines. Don't lead the crowd to give you a specific answer. Mindsharing needs as many possible answers in order to reveal the best answer. Keep this clear in your mind.

Here's an example of two different ways to ask the same question. The first question is about trying to lead the crowd, the second question is about getting the wisdom of the crowd. Both questions may lead to the same answer, but only the second question is true Mindsharing.

1. I think that it's time to upgrade my phone. As a big fan of Apple products, it's probably going to be a new iPhone. What do you think?

2. I think that it's time to upgrade my phone. The most important thing for me is that it's fast and has a good camera. What do you think?

MARKETING. Don't ask a question for the sake of marketing. Many brands will ask rather stupid questions from their crowd—not because they are looking for answers or crowd wisdom, but because they are trying to promote something. For example, Oreo might ask the crowd, "How do you like to eat your Oreo cookie?" Now there's a good chance they are not looking for innovative ideas to make huge advancements in cookie eating. They are marketing. They are seeing how many people will comment, not really looking for wisdom within the comments. People know when a question is genuine, whether you are Mindsharing for yourself or for a brand. Be authentic in your Mindsharing questions and you will get authentic results.

WHY DO PEOPLE CARE?

What motivates people to Mindshare?

Evolutionary biology shows that our brains are wired for connection, and that social connection is as fundamental to our survival as food and shelter. Matthew Lieberman, director of UCLA's Social Cognitive Neuroscience Lab and author of *Social: Why Our Brains Are Wired to Connect,* says that "just as there are multiple social networks on the Internet such as Facebook and Twitter, each with its own strengths, there are also multiple social networks in our brains, sets of brain regions that work together to promote our social well-being." These networks include the ability to bond with others, the ability to interpret the feelings of others, and the ability to be a harmonious part of a group. Our brains have developed these abilities in order to ensure our survival, and Lieberman says these "social adaptations are central to making us the most successful species on earth." Perhaps, in the not so distant future, people will be hooked up to functional MRI machines while they Mindshare, and neuroscience will show that Mindsharing is one of our best ways to also be our most successful selves.

I think we are also wired to connect in our hearts, and we

need one another for more than just survival. We all want to feel that we have meaningful value to give to others, and that we have an ability to influence others and the world. Our greatest natural resource is one another. We don't need natural disasters to come together as friends and communities. With Mindsharing and with our ability to be connected to one another, across the globe, at any given time, we have access to a way of collaborating like never before.

Mindsharing works because we are all deeply connected. And my struggle to make my dream come true is your struggle to make your dream come true. My quest to find love is the same as your quest to find love. My desire to save money when I buy a car or get a mortgage is the same as yours. Every parent wants the best for their child. When we share our struggles, we share our solutions. When we reach a hand out, there is always a hand reaching back. Always. This is why Mindsharing works so powerfully. We have a fundamental drive to be connected, to be in cooperation, and to contribute to a better world. Mindsharing provides us with the tools, the technologies, and a way to be in connection and cooperation with one another, and to help one another create better lives.

6.

CROWD CREATIVITY

(Mining the Collective Wisdom
for Creative Gold)

So far, we've discussed Mindsharing as a way to get collective intelligence—crowd wisdom that is comparable to expert wisdom. The methodology for this is simple. You look for a consensus from the crowd—the answer that most minds are suggesting is the best answer. If it's a numeric question (like guessing the weight of an ox), it's a calculated average or median. If it's an open question (like what car should I buy), it's the most common answer.

Wikipedia is a great example of a consensus platform. In Wikipedia, when there is disagreement among the Wikipedians (people who create the articles) they use consensus to make group decisions about the content of the article. This represents the collective intelligence of those who write and edit the information. Together, the crowd creates Mindsharing gold through agreement.

There is another strategy and methodology for Mindsharing that is utilized not when you are looking for crowd consensus or the best decision, but when you are looking for one creative idea. If you have Mindshared with your crowd and you have a small number of answers, it's simply a matter of reading through the ideas and deciding which one is best—which one jumps out at you as a brilliant and creative new idea. (You can then take this idea and ask for consensus from the crowd as to both its brilliance and creativity.) But what if you have hundreds of ideas? Thousands of ideas? How do you sift through them to find that one hidden gem?

You need a sieve to separate out the good from the bad, or the relevant from the irrelevant. If you have a good crowd (we will discuss when good crowds go bad in the next chapter), the crowd will self-monitor and filter the ideas by either clicking the "like" button or up-voting (depending on the platform) a particular idea or innovation.

When I Mindshared with my Facebook crowd for a creative idea for my TED talk, I received hundreds of suggestions. I immediately filtered out the ones that no one in the crowd showed interest in—those with no "likes." In most cases, the crowd ignores the irrelevant or bad ideas. There is no "dislike" button on Facebook, so we have to infer the uninterest of the crowd when a comment is ignored.

I then went back to the crowd with the two top ideas, and Mindshared for their consensus about which was a better idea.

A NEW WAY TO INNOVATE

This approach to finding creative ideas and solutions is not limited to individuals. Many corporations are using this strategy (often called open innovation) to get new product ideas or find solutions to problems. Procter & Gamble is one of the most experienced and long-term leaders of open innovation. In 2001, it launched a platform called "Connect + Develop." This platform allows P&G to crowdsource for creativity and innovation, and as a result, thousands of new products have been developed. By publishing a list of what it is looking for—this could be a new product, a new way of manufacturing something, or a creative idea for packaging—Procter & Gamble calls its program an "open door to the world" and receives more than four thousand creative ideas a year from this pioneering form of Mindsharing.

Instead of having a big crowd that votes on the creative idea or innovation, large organizations such as Procter & Gamble typically form a group of experts to evaluate and rate ideas. In addition, the ideas submitted are not made public, ensuring that the organization can leverage ideas, buy and own the intellectual property, and compete in the market. In this form of corporate Mindsharing, there are understandable concerns from the crowd about a big company "stealing" an idea from the crowd, and concerns from the company that the idea being submitted actually is the intellectual property of the person who is submitting the idea. For this reason, P&G will view only submissions that have intellectual property protections, which may include a trademark or a patent.

Idea Bounty (www.ideabounty.com) is another Mindsharing platform seeking creativity from the crowd. The site was started by two marketing executives after Jeff Howe wrote about crowdsourcing for *Wired* magazine.[1] Struggling with how to come up with creative ideas for their clients, they decided to turn to the crowd for a much larger creative pool. Idea Bounty was created not only as a resource for their creative needs, but as a portal for other companies to crowdsource creativity. It's a way for a company to work with thousands of "creatives" at one time, something that would usually be incredibly prohibitive for a company's bottom line. At Idea Bounty, companies give a description explaining the problem in need of a creative solution. People send their ideas in response to the company's brief. If your idea is used, the company pays the predetermined "bounty" or reward offered for the best creative idea or solution. Idea Bounty calls itself a social think tank for inspiration, and has a number of big-name corporate clients (think BMW, Chevrolet, and Red Bull). This type of Mindsharing for creativity hasn't been shown to have any downsides, and it does allow the crowd to choose projects that inspire them and helps companies broaden their creative reach. As we discussed with the site Fiverr, people who may not get paid to be creative in their nine-to-five job can still work on creative projects that used to be kept behind the closed doors of advertising agencies and marketing companies. The type of Mindsharing that Idea Bounty is using (along with other companies such as GeniusRocket, Victors & Spoils, crowd-SPRING, and DesignCrowd) is helping to usher in a new era of creativity—making it transparent, accessible, and affordable.

Other companies are letting the crowd build upon the creative ideas of one another to determine the best, most creative idea or story. Amazon Studios (studios.amazon.com) allows screenwriters to post their screenplays and has the crowd decide which premises and scripts should be made into a feature-length movie. They also invite the crowd to help develop the project along the way. By inviting creative talent and engaging the crowd in the process, the hope is that the final result will be better movies, more meaningful stories.

Time will tell.

Another Web site worth mentioning is 99designs (www.99designs.com), a crowdsourced platform for creative design. A big crowd of hobbyists and professional designers offer their design ideas for logos, business cards, and even book covers. As I was writing this chapter, I decided to do an experiment and created a brief asking the crowd to design a cover for this book. 99designs set the price of $299 for the winning designer.

I received dozens of designs. A key part of the creative development happened when I was asked to give feedback for each design. This dialogue is essential to the creative process when you are Mindsharing for creativity.

I showed the designs to my crowd, and the favorite design came from a designer named Lance Deacon. It's a brain created from the names of those who helped create this book.

Clever.

Creative.

I would never have thought of it on my own.

The 99designs cover is on the next page.

I showed the crowd this design and the design from my publisher. I posted a Facebook status and asked them for their collective recommendation. With more than five hundred comments and suggestions, this was the biggest engagement I have had while creating this book.

This crowdsourced cover was great, but there was also a great cover from the publisher. After using one methodology to come up with the cover on page 100, I went back to the crowd to use consensus to choose which of the two designs was better. Fifty-two percent chose the design you see on the cover of the book, and 43 percent voted for the design on the next page. It was a very tight competition, and both designs had passionate supporters. A few hours after I Mindshared for a consensus from my crowd, I received a private message in Facebook:

"Hi Lior. I am Lance Deacon, the designer who designed the cover you like. But my real name is not Lance Deacon. I'm actually one of your Facebook friends."

This came as a big surprise. I had a long chat with "Lance," and he explained that he used to be a professional designer,

MIND SHARING

The Art of Crowdsourcing Everything

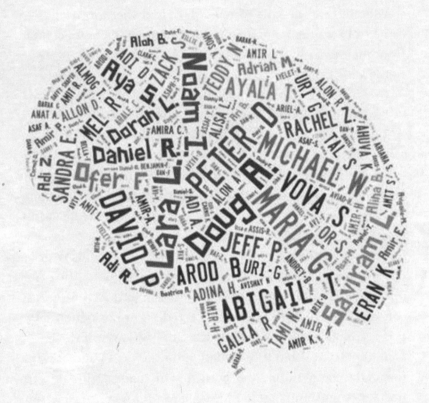

LIOR ZOREF

but then gave it up to pursue his dream of becoming an entrepreneur. He told me he's still passionate about design, so whenever he has some time, he designs on 99designs to keep in shape as a designer. This is his hobby. He shared with me his passion for a future where you don't have to have an expensive office and a big name in order to be a winning designer. "Great design starts with a big idea, and good ideas can come from anyone. I love the fact that on 99designs anyone can compete on projects in an absolutely objective way, without letting elements such as name, location, or reputation influence the customer's final choice. Only the quality of your work counts, so it must speak for itself. This is a new area, and I believe we will see this happening in more and more professional fields."

Mindsharing for creative ideas is an evolving methodology, and is not without its challenges. There are some who say that Web sites such as 99designs make designers work without getting paid (unless their design is chosen), while others see it as a disruptive force offering a cheap alternative to expensive designers. Without a doubt, it gives designers a chance to develop their portfolio and bid on jobs they might never have had access to without the platform.

Mindsharing for creative ideas also provides companies access to a greater pool of creative talent than they could ever afford in-house, and typically at a significantly reduced cost. For designers who are eager for work, and companies that are eager for more creative talent, Mindsharing for creativity can be a winning endeavor for all.

Seeking out an innovative idea, a never-before-found solution, or a new approach to an old problem is easy when you Mindshare. When we think together we are smarter, but we are also more creative. Creativity is about more than originality, it's also about functionality. We need to think of new ideas that work. New inspiration that is effective. Innovation that makes our lives easier and more joyful. We think of creative people as people who are full of unique ideas, original thinking. Creativity has always been somewhat of a mystery: some people hold the key to the treasure, some do not. This is the old model.

Mindsharing enables us all to be more creative—in our work life and in our personal life.

7.

WHEN GOOD CROWDS GO BAD
(When and Why Mindsharing Is Not Working)

Yossi Vardi is a famous Israeli entrepreneur, investor, and a really nice guy. In 2012, Yossi was the moderator for the closing session of the Chief Scientist's Annual Conference for Research and Development. The program promised that in this last session, "Speakers on the forefront of technological development will give dynamic and concise opinions on new trends." Yossi asked me to be on the panel, and my title in the program said "Crowd Wisdom Advocate."

No pressure.

I wanted to demonstrate crowd wisdom in real time for this audience. An ox was out of the question, so I decided to see whether crowd wisdom could guess the weight of a person.

Yossi volunteered to be that person.

Did I mention that Yossi is a bit chubby?

He is also a great sport.

He stood at the center of the stage and slowly turned in a circle so the crowd could get a view of him in all his glory. Each person guessed his weight, and I quickly calculated an estimated average.

Then, with the crowd's answer in hand, I dramatically turned to Yossi for the reveal. I asked him if the crowd was right, had they accurately guessed his weight?

Drumroll, please.

Yossi slowly shook his head. No. The crowd had not guessed his weight. They weren't even close. It was the first time that crowd wisdom had failed me. Yossi was happy, because it was obvious the crowd thought he weighed much less than he did, and while this made the audience laugh, I was puzzled and confused.

I was not happy at all.

After the panel session ended, I was anxious to understand why the experiment had failed. I asked a few people what their estimate had been. They immediately apologized and said, "We're sorry. We didn't want to embarrass him in public by guessing his real weight."

An embarrassed crowd is quite rare, and the failure of this crowd was my own failure. The crowd had failed at guessing Yossi's weight, but they had imparted their own wisdom into the experiment.

Don't publicly embarrass someone in service to an idea, even if he happily volunteers to participate.

Yossi and I had thought the whole experiment would be funny. The crowd taught us otherwise. They had refused to play because I had made them uncomfortable.

Sometimes crowds do go bad, and in this chapter we will discuss the conditions in a crowd that will hinder Mindsharing.

Lesson number one: don't bring a man onstage and ask people to guess his weight.

WE'RE ALL NAKED UNDERNEATH
OUR CLOTHES

When I was a child, I loved fairy tales. My favorite was "The Emperor's New Clothes" by Hans Christian Andersen. When I first read the story, I was caught up in the idea of clothing that was invisible to anyone unworthy of seeing it. Then I came to the part where the little boy yells out from the crowd, "But he isn't wearing anything at all!" I was so puzzled by this and surprised. How could it be that no one in this large crowd of people saw that the emperor was naked? The question stayed on my mind for years. Even at a young age, it seemed unreasonable that a big crowd would do something so stupid.

As I grew up, I learned that crowds could in fact be unreasonable, stupid, and even dangerous.

As a teenager I read William Golding's *Lord of the Flies*, in which a group of young British boys stuck on an uninhabited island try to govern themselves but descend into savagery. As a teenager, I also learned that in Nazi Germany, the people chose Hitler in a democratic election.

As an adult, I wondered why no one saw the dot-com bubble. And how is it that so many people still smoke cigarettes even knowing they kill? All around me, from childhood to adulthood, there were examples of large groups being horribly, disastrously, and dangerously wrong.

Pretending a man isn't naked is not crowd wisdom.

Descending into mob mentality is not crowd wisdom.

Professing that growth over profitability is a suitable business model is not crowd wisdom.

Nazi Germany was not crowd wisdom.

Sometimes good crowds go bad, and when this happens, the

result is not Mindsharing and crowd wisdom—it is exactly the opposite: herd stupidity.

MANIPULATE THIS

One of the most common reasons a good crowd goes bad is because there is manipulation within the crowd. Manipulation happens wherever there is the intention to influence the crowd or direct its behavior. We see this happen in advertising when brands try to manipulate consumers. We see this in the financial markets when people with interest in the stock try to manipulate its value. And we see this in regimes around the world where free speech and independent thought are not allowed. If you are Mindsharing and there is someone trying to sway the crowd to their particular thinking, the results will be tainted and unreliable. Your crowd must consist of independent individuals with a diversity of opinions. It is the intelligence and knowledge of each individual in a crowd that collectively creates better decision making, or an expert solution to a problem, or an innovative idea. Mindsharing is not about someone trying to sway the jury. You don't want someone's opinion or idea to be determined by the opinion or idea of another person. Successful Mindsharing depends on people thinking together, not being coerced into thinking alike.

SPY VS. SPY

One afternoon I received a mysterious phone call. The woman on the other end of the line had a low, Mata Hari type of voice.

Or so I imagined. She invited me to come speak to her group. When I asked her about the group, she paused and said it was a "group of government executives."

I thanked her for the invitation and asked her to send me an e-mail with all the details—my usual protocol for speaking engagement requests. This, however, was not the usual protocol for her group.

"We don't have e-mail. Can I send you a fax?"

A fax? No e-mail? Had I fallen asleep and woken up in 1985? Who doesn't have e-mail? I quickly set up a free online fax account and awaited her fax (which, ironically, would be forwarded to me via e-mail).

After receiving the fax, the details of which I'm not at liberty to reveal (if I told you, I'd have to kill you sort of thing), it became clear that I was being invited to speak to an intelligence agency. I can't name them, but suffice it to say that I do live in Israel and there is an institution here whose motto translates in English to "Where no counsel is, the people fall, but in the multitude of counselors there is safety."

A multitude of counselors? Sounds like a perfect place for Mindsharing.

For one day, I was going to be Bond, James Bond. I was a bit anxious as I traveled to speak to this group. What would they want to know? What would they ask me to do? I imagined they might give me a suitcase full of gadgets, a fully equipped spy car, and a briefcase of classified documents that only a Mindsharing Master could be privy to. Would I have to relocate my family? Would we go under government protection? How would I fight off all the beautiful female counteragents who might try to seduce information out of me?

Did I mention I have an overactive imagination at times?

The talk itself hardly lived up to my fantasy, but I shared the theory of crowd wisdom and presented a talk about Mindsharing. There was one question, however, that I hadn't encountered in any of my other talks: is it possible to manipulate crowd wisdom? In the months following this talk, I had some interesting discussions with other intelligence agencies and they all posed this same question.

In the traditional intelligence world, in order to get information, a spy was sent undercover with a fake name, a fake identity, and a detailed and false backstory. Creating this cover story requires a big effort, but it is and always has been what espionage is all about.

The question on the spy table now seems to be whether it is possible to create big crowds made up of individuals with fake identities and make them a part of real communities using social networks and other digital platforms. Is this how you can manipulate crowd wisdom secretly?

I don't imagine it's easy to do, but I imagine that there are countries and intelligence agencies who are trying to do just this. When it comes to spy vs. spy, there will always be people trying to use powerful media to their own advantage. With every new technology and every large and powerful crowd, there comes the inherent danger of manipulation. We just need to be aware. Be on the lookout for manipulation in our own crowds and in anonymous crowds.

If you have any questions, just shoot me an e-mail.

Or, if you're from a government agency, just send a fax and mark it to my attention.

The name is Zoref, Lior Zoref.

FACEBOOK, DON'T FAIL ME

Assuming we're not considering world domination or trying to discover state secrets, let's take a closer look at how Mindsharing can go wrong in our immediate networks. First, let's make sure our social network contains the criteria for crowd wisdom. Is it diverse enough, free of manipulation, and do we have a mechanism for aggregation (a way to determine the wisdom)?

Wikipedia built its own aggregation mechanism which allows Wikipedians to hold conversations, track changes, and make collective decisions. In Mindsharing, the aggregation mechanism is much simpler—it's comments. In Facebook, these are the comments posted in response to a status update. In Twitter it's the replies you get to a particular tweet. In a blog or a Q&A platform, it's the comments made on each post you make.

The advantage of this mechanism for aggregation is that it's quite simple and it's easy to engage and interact with the crowd. The disadvantage is that if you have a large number of responses, as we discussed earlier, it can take some time and effort in order to aggregate the information and discern the collective intelligence.

In order to have a diverse crowd we need to have a big crowd. If you are Mindsharing in a closed group of five of your best friends from college, this is not a diverse enough crowd and you are not going to get a range of independent thought. If we have a big enough crowd in Facebook, it will usually also be a diverse crowd. It may be made up of friends from college, from work, from high school, distant relatives, and friends of friends of friends. That's why I say you need approximately 250 people to form a large enough crowd for Mindsharing. If you have this many people at minimum, they will have diverse backgrounds, experience, ages, geography, and a wide range of specific knowledge. This is the first factor in a crowd that doesn't go bad.

The next criterion is independent thinking. If I post a question on Facebook, usually the only person going through the trouble of reading all the answers is me. Someone may read a few of the answers and give their own, but for the most part people answer independently of the other answers. It is fair to say that the answers are not influenced by others and people are thinking independently. This makes it hard to manipulate the responses (unless we ask a leading question).

In a social network such as Facebook, there is also less manipulation because people are not anonymous. Any comment usually comes with a name, a picture, and a certain level of transparency because in order to comment they have to have been accepted into your network. Anonymity breeds manipulation because people are not held accountable for their speech or, as we see in many cases in public comments, their sales pitch. How many times have you been reading through a comment string and someone has posted a link to a product he or she is selling, or otherwise posted something that clearly shows a personal agenda? Often these comments can seem to be genuine at first, but then stray into "and then I made lots of money working from home" or some other piece of "wisdom."

This isn't to say there can't be manipulation without anonymity.

After all, Hitler was certainly anything but anonymous. We're not talking about groupthink, mass hysteria, or the propaganda of dictators. Mindsharing is a democracy, and as such it allows for free speech, but the crowd, as do the people, will usually self-monitor and self-correct when one particular person

tries to turn crowd wisdom into his or her own personal soap-
box or platform for manipulating the rest of the crowd. In most
cases, in a social network with identified members, the required
conditions for crowd wisdom are met and the result will be
crowd wisdom rather than groupthink or herd stupidity. If you
ask the question in the wrong way, or your crowd is too small,
or someone is trying to manipulate the answer, then look out
for the virtual equivalent of a *Lord of the Flies*–type quest for
power and control. If your crowd starts resorting to savagery,
build a signal fire, keep your head down, and hope the British
troops arrive soon to save you.

Or you can simply delete the post, evaluate where you've
failed to meet the criteria for crowd wisdom, and try again.
When the crowd goes bad, whether you are Mindsharing as an
individual or Mindsharing as a company, you always have the
option of pulling the plug on your Mindsharing endeavor and
going back to the drawing board.

PART 3

MINDSHARE YOUR PERSONAL LIFE

8.

SMART MONEY
(Using the Crowd to Mind Your Money)

Rule No. 1: Never lose money.

Rule No. 2: Don't forget rule No. 1.

WARREN BUFFETT

Nobody likes to lose money. Warren Buffett's advice is great, but how do we follow Rule No. 1? How do we navigate the manipulative waters of advertising, search engines, and brand propaganda? The Internet makes it easy to research almost any product we can imagine buying, but often the results are skewed, biased, and funded by the very companies we are researching. Even something as simple as searching for a hotel on Google mostly results in other Web sites that are trying to sell you that hotel. Even more insidious, you and I can both type the exact same query into the same search engine and get different results.

Not very comforting.

Is it any wonder that consumers are turning more and more to word of mouth and (hopefully) unbiased reviews from other consumers? In the digital age, we have lost our trust in most brands and their advertising, but with Mindsharing, we have a trusted tool to help us make the best possible and most educated decisions when paying for a service or a product. This gets us all closer to following Warren Buffett's number one rule.

MAGIC SHOES

I was fourteen years old and I needed new shoes. Now, don't get me wrong, I had shoes, but I just didn't have the right kind of shoes, the "cool" kind of shoes. I needed magic shoes. Shoes that would transform me from the shy, geeky boy more at home in front of his Apple II computer than in front of real people (fourteen-year-old girl kind of people, to be exact) into a cool, confident guy. My parents were worried about me, and thought I needed to be more "social" and have more friends. I didn't know how to go about being social or how to gather friends. The entire concept felt awkward and embarrassing.

I was happiest in front of my computer.

My parents insisted, however, so I began working at a local mall to earn money to buy the shoes that I imagined would make me less geeky and more "social." As I mentioned earlier, it was a retail computer store, so I still found a way to be around computers all day.

After working hard and saving harder, I took my entire life savings (one hundred dollars) and spent it on the cool pair of shoes I had seen all the popular kids at school wearing. Needless to say, I wasn't magically transformed like some geeky Cinderella by these shoes. In fact, by the time I had saved up and bought the shoes, all the cool kids were wearing a different style of shoes altogether.

I went back to my Apple II, without any new friends and without having learned the secrets of socializing. My one regret was spending my life savings on an outdated pair of shoes. Today, if I need to know how to spend my money I have a crowd of friends (bigger than anything I could ever have imagined when I was fourteen) to help me make my spending decisions. I also have a crowd that is there to guide me back to reality when I think any product will offer some sort of magical solution to a problem. I still spend my days in front of a computer screen, but I am more connected and more social than ever.

My parents are no longer worried.

Once you've built your network, or learned how to tap into existing networks (as we discussed in Part One), you can use the crowd to mind your money. On Quora, a fourteen-year-old boy posted a question (under the topic "Stock Market") regarding how to invest his life savings. Here is his post:

As a 14-year-old, how should I invest my life savings of $800?

I'm just going to put it out there—I'm 14. I have my whole life ahead of me, and that's what sets me apart from all the other investors—I have time. Lots of it. 30 years, 50 years, heck, since we're living longer, 80 years of letting my money grow, grow, grow. Because I have so much time, what is the best way to invest my life savings of $800 to grow over time?

The boy went on to list various possibilities within the stock market and asked the crowd for both help and inspiration.

What was the most common answer he received from Mindsharing? The answer he received from this mixed crowd (not all financial experts) was *not* to invest his money at all. Instead, the crowd told him to use the money to create a small business and "learn how to build relationships." He was also advised to save up until he was sixteen and buy a car. The crowd went on to advise him that "car ownership is the highest predictor of whether someone can get a job" and a car would "increase his ability to socialize and network" as well as be an asset if he were to run his own business. By Mindsharing, this boy not only was able to make a better decision about what to do with his life savings, he was given valuable advice for his future. When it comes to our money, Mindsharing is a way to get valuable crowd wisdom that results in bias-free financial advice.

NOT A CAR GUY

When I retired from Microsoft (and turned in the company car), I found myself faced with the daunting task of buying a new car. I know nothing about cars. For me a car is just a tool to get me from point A to point B.

Since buying a car is an important (and expensive) decision, I found myself struggling to decide. I was overwhelmed with the choices, the options, and the financing, and wary of car salespersons in general. One of my friends is an expert in this field and I tried to ask his advice, but his response was too complicated and full of terms that I didn't know or even want to know.

Instead of listening to advertising or trying to understand my friend, the expert, I turned to the crowd. This is what I wrote on my Facebook page: "I'm looking to buy a new car for me and my family. I don't care about the car brand. I only need it to be safe, efficient, and easy to maintain. What do you think?"

After an hour or so, I received more than a hundred responses. As I was going through their recommendations, I saw that many in my crowd were car hobbyists or people who had the same criteria for buying a new car. When you ask a big crowd something, the people who choose to respond are usually those who feel they have enough knowledge or experience in the subject matter to give an intelligent response. I'm not a car guy—but apparently, many in my crowd were.

I grouped all the answers with similar recommendations. Someone suggested that I get a Segway, but I was looking for the collective intelligence of the group as a whole and not just one crazy idea.

The group with the largest number of similar responses recommended I buy a Hyundai i30cw. This was the collective answer from the majority, so this is what I considered to be the collective crowd intelligence. The crowd told me this particular vehicle was a great family car, dependable, less expensive than some bigger brands, and as a result, the best value for the money. After less than twenty-four hours, I bought the Hyundai based on the wisdom of my crowd.

A few weeks later, I met with the editor of the automobile section in one of the largest newspapers in Tel Aviv. I told him my criteria and asked him what car he would recommend. His advice—the Hyundai i30cw.

Score one for Mindsharing.

In the end, I didn't have to do a lot of research on various car-buying sites. I didn't have to trust the slick car salesman. I didn't have to try to understand a lot of technical specifications or automotive language. I just had to ask the crowd. By doing so, I saved time and money, and was able to make an informed decision in less than two hours. More important, the very next day I was driving my new red Hyundai. Anyone who has spent days, weeks, possibly months researching and test-driving cars knows the profound savings I experienced in simply asking the crowd.

Mindsharing, however, is not limited to just automobile purchases. It works for virtually every financial decision, big or small. My good friend Yosi got married a few years ago. In

Israel, immediately after you get married, you are expected to buy a house and have children. Immediately. So Yosi went to the bank to take out a mortgage, which is a bit like a marriage, just more expensive.

The mortgage broker told him, "I have an amazing deal for you, but it's just for today!" Yosi listened to the broker, took out his phone, and wrote on his Facebook wall the details of the offer. He then asked, "Is this a good deal?"

The broker didn't know what Yosi was doing on his phone. She smiled at him, told him about their new coffee machine, and offered him a fresh cup of coffee. Yosi was polite and smiled back, but he was more interested in seeing what his crowd had to say about the "amazing deal."

A few minutes later, as he drank a great cup of coffee, the answer from his crowd was a resounding "No way!" His crowd also shared with him the terms they had received when they had gotten mortgages. When he relayed this to the mortgage broker, she gave him an angry look and told him, "I don't know who these people are. I don't know their terms or financial backgrounds. If you had their formal mortgage offers, then I could respond."

Yosi went back to his wall and wrote, "The bank needs to see documents with your offers. Can you please send them to the bank's fax number?" Yosi listed the number, and within ten minutes, the mortgage broker was inundated by mortgage documents. Through Mindsharing, Yosi used crowd wisdom to learn that the bank's coffee was a whole lot better than its mortgages.

Building a retirement plan, taking out a mortgage, and other financial decisions are very complex to understand. There are many experts who are willing to "help out," but in many cases these experts are working not for your best interests but for those of their employer or the companies they represent.

Mindsharing helps you get unbiased and expert advice for all the important financial decisions you have to make in life.

I am happy to say that Yosi is both happily married and happily mortgaged.

FRAUD PREVENTION

If we follow the number one rule of never losing money—we have to not only look at our spending choices so we are not paying higher prices, but also make sure we are not losing money by becoming one of the approximately thirteen million people a year (U.S.) who fall victim to credit card fraud.[1] Let's explore how Mindsharing can help us with both scenarios.

Suzanne Brenner was preparing to leave on a trip from New York to St. Louis when she discovered something startling and disturbing—fraudulent charges on her debit card. There were three unrecognizable charges for $29.99 each. It wasn't a large amount, and after wracking her brain to see if she had some purchases she might have forgotten about and coming up with nothing, she called her bank to look into the charges. Her bank had no answers about the charges, and ended up patching her through to the fraud department. They could give her no more specifics about who had authorized the charges or what they were for; all they could do was immediately cancel her card. Suzanne scrambled to find an alternate card to use for her trip to St. Louis.

This was not the first time that Brenner had fallen victim to credit card fraud. The year before, someone had fraudulently made close to thirty-five separate unauthorized charges on her debit card. Most of those charges were for small amounts of money—$9.99 or less—so she ignored them. She assumed her statements were reflecting unplanned purchases that had just skipped her mind—a bagel and coffee here or there, a subscription she had forgotten about. Those unauthorized charges had run rampant for almost eight months before she caught on and canceled her card.

After she returned from St. Louis and told a former colleague about the fraudulent charges and the hassle of not having her debit card on her trip, he recommended that she try a new crowdsourced service called BillGuard (www.billguard.com). This service will automatically find and alert you to deceptive (think of the free trial that converts to a paid subscription, or the "accidental" times when an online company bills you repeatedly for the same purchase) or fraudulent charges on your credit card. These types of charges, collectively called "gray charges," cost American consumers almost $14 billion annually.[2]

Mindsharing is providing a way for people to help one another financially. By aggregating the information from a large crowd of fraud victims, Mindsharing can reach a consensus that will alert other potential fraud victims immediately. This information is already out there. Every day tens of thousands of people report fraudulent charges to their bank or credit card company, and the next day tens of thousands of people can potentially get the same charge on their card. Without Mindsharing, it may be a month or longer before those people even know about the fraud. With Mindsharing, crowd wisdom can be shared instantly and used to save people time, money, and a whole lot of headaches.

Will Mindsharing make credit card fraud go away? No, but it does help consumers take back some of the control that is lost. Eventually, once a company is tagged enough as fraudulent it will cease doing business. Hopefully the crowd's collective data will be used by law enforcement to either stop the fraudsters or prevent fraud from happening in the future. Mindsharing allows millions of fraud victims and credit card users to come together and share their collective wisdom. It enables us to connect and help one another financially.

Suzanne joined the crowd at BillGuard and immediately got an e-mail alerting her to suspicious charges on her new card. It didn't take months, and she didn't have to wrack her brain or spend hours on the phone with banks and merchants. She could take action immediately. This is Mindsharing at its collective finest—helping you to protect your money by harnessing the collective intelligence and experience of others.

Warren Buffett would be proud.

INVESTING IN MINDSHARING

We've discussed how to use Mindsharing to avoid losing money when making big purchasing decisions, and how to use Mindsharing to prevent money loss from fraudulent charges—but can Mindsharing also prevent you from losing money in the stock market? Can Mindsharing actually predict the stock market?

Stock market predictions are known to be about as accurate as a coin toss. Children and monkeys have proven to do just as well as (or even better than) experts. In 1973, Professor Burton Malkiel from Princeton University claimed, "A blindfolded monkey throwing darts at a newspaper's financial pages could select a portfolio that would do just as well as one carefully selected by experts." He was correct. In some cases, the blindfolded monkeys even outperformed the experts.[3]

I'm no stock market expert, but I do know that in general

the stock market is based on a mechanism that reflects the collective expectations of the investors and the public. In a perfect world—a world without manipulation—this means that the stock market performs in alignment with the hive mind (when two or more independent people come to the same thought or conclusion at the same time and they do not know each other). In the case of the stock market, the hive mind is our collective expectation of how the market will perform.

In 2008, researchers from Indiana University began with the theory that the rise and fall of the stock market is a reflection of the mood of the public, or the hive mind. To test this theory, they turned to Twitter. Analyzing almost ten million tweets from close to three million "tweeters" using an algorithm called the Google Profile of Mood States (GPOMS), they tested it to understand the mood of the hive mind. They found that one of the moods the algorithm tests for—calmness—had a direct correlation with the stock market. Their findings were that the calmness index could predict whether the stock market will go up or down. When the hive mind is calm, the stock market goes up approximately six days later. When the hive mind is not calm, the stock market goes down. Their Twitter analysis could predict the Dow Jones Industrial Average with 87.6 percent accuracy.[4]

Blindfolded monkeys throwing darts are no match for the collective mood of the hive mind.

BACK TO WARREN BUFFETT

There is no doubt that Warren Buffett is the most successful investor in the world. His company Berkshire Hathaway has more money than it knows what to do with, and is the highest price per share stock on the New York Stock Exchange. As of October 2014, one share of stock in Berkshire Hathaway would cost you $206,393.[5] For one share. It's too rich for my blood, and I daresay probably too rich for many others as well.

I mentioned earlier that I'm no stock market expert. In fact, the stock market intimidates me. It is a complex machine run by select analysts and investment brokers who seem to have special skills and knowledge—an elite club with very limited transparency. Most investors don't even understand how their money is invested. Government agencies monitor the stock market and its activities, always on the watch for manipulation and insider trading. There is manipulation in the stock market (that's why the SEC exists), and when large amounts of money are on the line, the line can get crossed. Companies and stocks can be promoted or debunked online and in the media in order to affect a stock's value. Because one of the key requirements for Mindsharing is the ability to think without manipulation (nothing stops crowd wisdom in its tracks faster than manipulation), investing in the stock market through Mindsharing has been difficult. Difficult, but not impossible.

We could succeed as investors if we only invested in Warren Buffett and his company, although who has the financial resources to be a Warren Buffett? Instead, through Mindsharing, we don't need Warren Buffett.

We have Julio.

And we have eToro.

eToro.com (not yet available in the United States) is the world's first social trading and investment network. It is a platform (with a few Mindsharing elements) that "connects people to invest in the financial markets, share their financial strategies, and tap into the wisdom of crowds to make smarter investment decisions."[6]

Julio Rus Fernandez is a firefighter from Spain. Julio is twenty-eight years old and began investing part-time in the financial markets four years ago. Julio learned quickly that he is not only good at fighting fires; he is also good at investing. But you don't have to take Julio's word for it. Contrary to other trading platforms, at eToro anyone can see your portfolio and learn whether you've gained or lost in your investments. Total transparency. All trading information (except for the actual amounts) is public information. Whenever *anyone* buys or sells a stock on eToro, *everyone* can have access to the information and make their own analysis.

As Julio began to perform well in his trading, people began following him and copying his trades. At eToro you can decide to copy other investors based on their performance. When you copy someone, it means that you automatically buy and sell the same stocks as the person you copy.

Julio is now a popular investor, and at the time of writing this book, he has more than 140,000 followers and more than 4,500 people who copy his trades. eToro is not tapping into the full potential of Mindsharing, as investors still make their decisions alone. But the fact that many people choose to copy someone based on his performance makes it a crowd-based recommendation. eToro not only takes the guesswork and secrecy and manipulation out of stock market investing, it is ushering in a new era. When Mindsharing meets the stock market, a new generation of investors is born.

A few words of caution: Crowd wisdom does not mean that the crowd is always right, but that a crowd can be as smart as an expert. In the financial market, many experts fail, and the crowd can fail as well. Most experts failed to predict past market collapses (bubbles), and when you copy another trader, you can gain when he gains, but you can also lose when he loses. I'm not recommending that anyone invest in the stock market (I don't), but if you do, I am simply saying you can choose your risks based on insights from traditional experts and also from the crowd.

(For an updated list of Mindsharing resources for finance and funding, please go to mindsharing.info/finance.)

CROWDFUNDING

As I mentioned earlier, nothing will make your crowd disappear faster than trying to sell them something or hitting them up for money. Don't do it. Your social network is not a bank.

There is a crowd out there, however, that will support you not only in making smart financial decisions, but also in raising funds. One of the most exiting recent developments in the area of Mindsharing is called crowdfunding. Kickstarter (www.kick starter.com) and Indiegogo (www.indiegogo.com) are two of the leading crowdfunding platforms. These platforms (and there are many more) enable a new kind of funding. Anyone can publish a project or present a dream and ask for funds from a big crowd. Do you dream of making a movie or writing a novel? Present your dream to the crowd and see who wants to support you monetarily in its pursuit. There are even crowdfunded babies—cases where parents raised money for fertility treatments or adoption costs. Having a family is a dream for many, and crowdfunding helps make that dream, and so many other dreams, possible.

Mindsharing has the potential to help you spend your money more wisely, guard it more carefully, invest it more successfully, and raise it more expediently. Money may not be the answer to all our problems, but sometimes we get by with a little help from our friends.

9.

SMILE FOR THE CROWD
(Finding and Keeping Love with Mindsharing)

We have looked at how Mindsharing can help our financial decisions and affect our wallet, but what about our romantic decisions? Will it work just the same when it comes time to invest our hearts? We all want to love and be loved, and I daresay there is nothing that confounds us more, drives us crazier, or causes more turmoil in our lives than love. How do we find a date? What do we do on a date? How do we keep a relationship strong? How do we know if that special someone is "the one"? Is it possible that Mindsharing can help us both find and keep love?

LASAGNA AND LOVE

It was 1997 and my mother was freaking out. I didn't have children. I wasn't married. I didn't even have any prospects. Women scared me to death. Needless to say, my love life was a disaster.

My marketing career at Microsoft was just taking off, and most of my time was spent focusing on my job. I worked day and night, and felt very successful. Marketing I could understand and master, but women were a complete mystery. Deep down, I was incredibly lonely, but I never would have admitted this to my friends or family. My self-confidence was low, but I hid it behind my long hours at work and blamed my lack of a romantic life on my job.

I knew the love of my life was out there in the world somewhere, but I had no idea how to find her.

One day I was asked to give a presentation at a large Microsoft product launch. I would be onstage doing demos of the product and I was thrilled. It was a geek's dream come true. One of the most famous television and radio hosts in Israel, Avri Gilad, was hosting the event. He and I became friends as the rehearsals for the event progressed. One day he asked me a personal question: "Lior, my friend, do you have a girlfriend?"

I looked at him, surprised. Had my mother called him behind my back? Was she in fact secretly conspiring with all of Israel in order to someday have grandchildren, as I often suspected?

"No," I answered.

I didn't tell him that not only did I not have a girlfriend, I couldn't even remember the last time I had a date.

Unless you counted the woman I bought my coffee from every morning.

Did I mention I was twenty-seven years old?

Avri went on to ask me to join him on his popular radio show—a matchmaking show. There was no way I was going to go on the radio and admit that I was looking for a date. I couldn't think of anything more embarrassing than sharing what I saw as my complete romantic failure with a large audience.

Avri reassured me that I would have more dates than I would know what to do with and that I could use an alias. "No one will know it's you," he promised.

Eventually I agreed, and when the day of the radio show arrived, I was terrified and panicked. Nevertheless, I was also desperate enough in the female department, and curious enough about whether or not I would get a date or two, to go on the show.

Avri asked me to share some personal details about myself with his radio audience. One of the things I shared was that I loved to cook, and my specialty was lasagna.

Who knew that this little personal detail would open the female floodgates like never before in my life. Hundreds of women wanted to meet me and go on a date. Apparently, cooking lasagna made me "cute." If I had known this earlier, I would have cooked lasagna every single day of my life.

In the weeks that followed I had more dates than I could ever have imagined—sometimes as many as three in a single evening. Now, as an engineer, I know that I can solve most problems with an Excel spreadsheet, so a friend and I set up a spreadsheet for the hundreds of women I was dating. We sorted and rated all my dates. I tracked the cafés I met them in, what we talked about, how long the date lasted, and whether I thought we should see each other again. It was a crazy process, but with my spreadsheet I felt somewhat in control of the hundreds of blind dates I found myself going on.

On that radio show in 1997, I was Mindsharing without even knowing I was Mindsharing. I learned that by turning to a big crowd in my quest for love, I had more opportunities to find love. Today, more than a third of marriages begin online, and there are numerous dating Web sites where people can go to find love. But with Mindsharing, you don't have to go to a dating Web site or be a guest on a radio show under a fake name. With Mindsharing you can turn to your crowd and ask for help. It can be help with finding a date, or help with going on a date, or help with keeping your relationship or marriage thriving.

If you're looking for love through Mindsharing, the big question you must ask yourself is this: are you willing to admit it to your friends, colleagues, and family? Mindsharing can save you a lot of time in your quest for love, but only if you'll have the courage to do it publicly. With our immediate social networks, each of us has the equivalent of the dating radio show I went on. If you are willing to do anything, here's what you need to do:

ARTICULATE. First of all, open a blank word processing page and write down what you're looking for. Do not write your first draft on your social media site. Do not write it under the influence (friends don't let friends drink and post). Be honest and share why you are looking for love, where you have failed in the past, and what it means to you. It's always good to share a personal story that might help your weak ties get to know you better. If you have any conditions, such as a partner of a particular age, religion, geographical location, children or no children, state them up front. Make sure you let people know that they can contact you in a public comment but also privately (many people will be happy to help but prefer to do so privately).

SLEEP ON IT. Don't publish it right away. Take the time, go over your text, make sure that you're comfortable with what you wrote. Revise. Ask yourself if there's anything you wouldn't want your friends to know? Your family? Your colleagues? Your ex-girlfriend or ex-boyfriend? Think about your network and who it consists of. You also have the option (on Facebook) of changing the privacy settings if you wish to exclude a particular friend from reading your post. Read it to a trusted friend or family member and ask them for their comments.

PUBLISH. When you feel it's ready, you have a few options. You can post it as a Facebook status or a note. Notes give you the ability to title your post and also are a bit easier to edit. The bolder option is to publish it as a blog piece (create a new blog or add it to an existing blog). When you share your journey to find love on a blog, you open yourself to a bigger crowd, as blogs are indexed by Google. When people search Google for love, they might find your blog piece if you have "love" in the title. WordPress is a good option if you are creating a new blog, and you can get it designed (complete with pictures) and up and running in about thirty minutes.

BE CAUTIOUS. The Internet is full of wonderful people, and people who are not so wonderful. It's good to consider the fact that when you open yourself up to the crowd for connections, the crowd can't vet every connection you make, especially if you are looking for love recommendations outside of your immediate social network. Try to get as many details as you can about a potential date, especially if the degrees of separation between you are great. When you do transition from the digital world to the real world for a meeting or a date, meet somewhere in public, let your friends know where you are going and with whom, and trust your instincts.

Facebook has virtually eliminated the concept of "blind dates" and transformed the dating experience. If I wanted to go on a date today, I could look at the person's Facebook page and see what she looks like, who her friends are, where she grew up, went to school, and works, and even possibly see photos of her last boyfriend, and know from her relationship status and Timeline how long she has been single.

Assuming her privacy settings allow it.

Today, 49 percent of men and 55 percent of women restrict access to their personal information on Facebook.[1] In other words, approximately half of your efforts to "Facebook stalk" someone will fail.

And half will succeed.

Some would call this a blessing. Others may call it a curse. The reality is we rarely go on a date "blind" in the age of social media. Everything you want to know about a potential date is just a Google search or a Facebook profile away.

People are still searching, however, and still as confounded as ever in their quest for love. This is where Mindsharing comes in. With Mindsharing, you don't have to search endless profiles or become your own private investigator. You can simply ask your crowd. Your crowd can be your matchmaker. And as it turns out, the crowd can be just as skilled as any expert (and expensive) matchmaker or online dating site. They don't need complicated algorithms or for you to complete exhaustive psychological profiles to find your perfect match. Collectively the crowd has wisdom, and when you turn your love life over to the crowd, amazing things can happen.

EVERYONE IS A MATCHMAKER

For centuries, people have been outsourcing matchmaking to clergy or others (in a tribe or ancient culture) with the sacred job of connecting the right person with the right person. Now back in the day the right match might depend on exactly how many cattle grazed someone's land. Today things are a bit more complicated. In recent years, online dating Web sites have been using algorithms to match people, and it's not breaking news to say that these dating Web sites are very popular. According to a Pew Research study from 2013, 59 percent of Internet users in the United States think that online dating is a good way to meet people. But 54 percent also believe people "seriously misrepresent themselves in their online profile."[2]

Within our social networks, we have single friends or friends of friends. And each of us can be a matchmaker among our friends, or use our crowd for their potential matchmaking services. We just have to look again at Granovetter's "Strength of Weak Ties" theory. If it's true that our weak ties have more impact on finding us a job, could they also have more impact on helping us to find love? Because our strong ties know the same people we know, our chances are less that we will meet new people through them. Our weak ties, however, can connect us and be the bridge to entirely new networks of people and new opportunities for dating and love.

So why is it that when someone posts a status that he or she is looking for love, many of us engage and try to help? Why do people become matchmakers? We don't get a fee. According to a study from Duke University and Harvard Business School,[3] people who succeed in matchmaking, who successfully connect two people up, are happier. It's an act of altruism. When we find love it makes us happy. When we help others to find love, it also makes us happy.

Reut Frenkel is beautiful and talented. She was frustratingly single. Reut tried using online dating Web sites, hoping to find her Prince Charming, but according to Reut, all she ended up with was a whole lot of frogs. After many bad dates, where the person in front of her rarely matched the person he pretended to be on the dating site, Reut decided she would have a better chance of finding love using her Facebook friends. After much trepidation, she was brave enough to post the following status:

For those who know me, you will probably understand that this status is not easy for me to write. But if you can't beat them, join them. In my 32 years I've been blessed. Blessed with great family and many good friends. I enjoy my work and enjoy every single day of my life. Yet, I still haven't found the guy I will grow old with. The guy I will someday laugh with as we read this status when we are 80.

So, what do I want from you?

Maybe you know this guy and you forgot to introduce us. Or maybe he is just sitting out there somewhere, looking for me, and waiting to read this status. You can share this and you also know where to find me.

Tell him I'm waiting.

Reut's status was shared more than eight thousand times. Hundreds of men contacted her, and she found herself going on dates with men more interesting than any of those matched with her on dating sites. Her crowd had heard her, and had stepped in to help her in her quest for love.

It took a lot of courage for Reut to post that status, and she spent quite some time actively meeting her prospective matches and going on dates thanks to the crowd (eight thousand shares equals a lot of dates). Mindsharing certainly increased Reut's odds of finding love. It was the same when I went on the radio show. Even if you don't have a big crowd, if you are real, honest, and vulnerable, it will strike a chord and people will respond and share your status. Reut's post continues to reach far beyond her own Facebook crowd, and it may have reached the man she will laugh about this with her when she's eighty. As of this writing, Reut found love through Mindsharing, although she says it's still too early to know if it is the love of her life. The odds are good, and Reut says she doesn't regret putting her trust in the crowd.

A GUY WALKS INTO A BAR

I have no doubt that Mindsharing can compete with the most talented matchmaker on the planet when it comes to finding love. Crowdsourcing for romance involves a different level of vulnerability and trust in the crowd. It takes a certain kind of courage to tell your Facebook friends or Twitter followers that you are looking for love, or a date, or even a friend. But often when it comes to matters of the heart, our friends, our family, and even strangers can do for us what we cannot do for ourselves—see clearly.

When a friend of mine (who I will call David) was a student, he went into a bar with a good friend of his. They made a bet about who would buy dinner that evening. The bet was that David would go up to ten different women in the bar and ask them if they would sleep with him. If David got a yes from any of the ten women, his friend had to buy dinner. Now David was no Romeo. But he did know statistics. He approached ten women, politely asked them if they would like to sleep with him, and out of the ten, one did say yes. David not only got a free dinner out of the experience, he learned a valuable lesson. There was power in numbers. Now I don't recommend walking up to every woman you see and asking her to sleep with you (that is a sure way to either be slapped or arrested), but you can learn from David's experience.

Later in life, when David found himself looking for love, he remembered his experience in the bar and knew he needed big numbers—needed to reach as many women as possible in order to have the best chance of finding his true love and future wife. In what was for him a last-ditch attempt, David decided to use Mindsharing. He created a blog in which he relayed his journey and aspiration to be in love and build a family. Then he went to his crowd of friends and told them about this blog. People visited the Web site, empathized with and related to his search for love, appreciated his courage and honesty, and told single women they thought might be a good match to visit the site as well.

Eventually David found the perfect match. In his blog, when he described himself he wrote that he was a vegetarian. The woman who found him had done a simple Google search with the question, "How can I find a vegetarian date?" This led her to David's blog, and the rest is history. Today, he and the woman he met through his very open and public quest are happily married. If not for his honest Mindsharing, David might still be home waiting for Cupid to strike. Or he might still be striking out in bars all over town.

I FOUND A DATE, NOW WHAT?

Mindsharing is not just for finding a date; it can also help you out on your dates. Dating always made me nervous. It was like being in a high-pressure job interview, but for a job I wasn't even sure I wanted in the first place. I thought curing cancer might be easier than going on a date. There's no doubt that bad dates happen. They can happen whether you found your date through Mindsharing or from an online dating site, or whether your mother fixed you up with her best friend's sister's niece's cousin's next-door neighbor.

There is a new app called Lulu that makes me glad I'm happily married and not dating today. Lulu provides a platform for women to anonymously review and rate the men they date. It's like TripAdvisor, but instead of rating hotels you are rating your dates. Based on Lulu's secret algorithm and the hashtags women give their dates, the men end up with a score between 1 and 10. Hashtags include things such as #neversleepover, #pornedu-cated, #obsessedwithhismother, and #wanderingeye, or more posi-tive ones such as #dudecancook or #talldarkandhandsome.

A man in Brazil is currently suing Lulu because he didn't care for the comments (although he received a pretty high rat-ing).[4] Basically Lulu is doing online in a crowd what women have been doing forever—discussing and rating the men they encounter. Now they are just Mindsharing their observations. We'll see if Lulu survives the backlash from men, but for now, it is still going strong.

Just as we can use Mindsharing to get the date, we can also use Mindsharing to help us decide what to do on the date. If you Google "ideas for a first date," one of the first results you'll get is from a blog that advises you to "Wake up at four A.M. and watch the sunrise together." Mindsharing gives a completely different answer from the Google search. In Quora, someone posed the question: "What are some good ideas for things to do on a first date?" The crowd offered many suggestions. The most common suggestion was not to watch the sunrise at four A.M., but to go on a picnic. The crowd also offered suggestions about what *not* to do on a first date, including an expensive dinner, movies (where you can't have a conversation), and strip clubs. But if you need Mindsharing to tell you that a strip club is not the best idea for a first date, you may wish to consult the crowd for every dating decision you make in the future.

On Quora you can anonymously ask the crowd for dating advice on virtually every topic. Some people choose this more anonymous place for Mindsharing about their love lives rather than Facebook or Twitter. After all, do you really want your date to know you spent two days trying to decide what to wear on your first date? Or that you went to the crowd to see whether you should move in for the first kiss during the date or at the end of the date?

FIRST COMES LOVE,
THEN COMES MARRIAGE

So, you've Mindshared your way into a date, possibly even a relationship. Now what? Once we are in a relationship, we need to keep that relationship going—keep the fire burning, so to speak. Can Mindsharing make our relationships better? Easier? More satisfying?

The truth is, more than a third of all divorce filings in 2013 contained the word "Facebook."[5] Mark Zuckerberg changed his Facebook status to "married" in 2012, but Facebook is the reason many couples end up changing their status to "single." Reconnecting with past loves, the ability to friend someone you've just met, and the ability to interact in a personal way has been detrimental to many marriages. No one doubts that social media has the potential to hurt relationships, but Mindsharing can help your relationship, and it can also keep you from wasting your time on bad relationships, and even save you years of therapy.

MY HUSBAND IS A MORON

One of the best places to learn more about relationships is from the experiences of others. While researching this chapter, I looked for a big crowd of people who were Mindsharing different aspects of marriage, relationships, and parenthood. In the past, forums seemed to be the place where big crowds discussed different topics and shared their experiences. Now Facebook groups are the popular replacement for forums.

The problem is many of these Faccbook groups are closed. You have to be a member. There are criteria for membership. Many people told me about one particular Facebook group that was engaging in powerful Mindsharing on the topic of parenting *and* relationships, and touching the lives of tens of thousands of people.

I desperately wanted to join this group.

There was one problem.

It was a group for women only.

No. Men. Allowed.

I did something I am not proud of. I used the Facebook account of a woman I knew in order to look around this group and see if there was something I could learn and share in this chapter. To my surprise, the first post I saw was the following:

"My husband is a moron!"

I was shocked. How and why would someone write this? It wasn't anonymous—anyone in the group could see this person's name and profile picture. And by default, could know the identity of her husband (the alleged moron).

Was this what women did in their private groups? It was my worst fear realized, and on behalf of all moronic husbands everywhere, I was outraged.

I then started to peek at the comments this woman received on her post, and to my continued surprise, many other women said, "You are right. My husband is a moron, too!" The women all seemed to agree that their husbands were morons, but they also went on to agree, "We wouldn't replace him with anyone else."

It became obvious that this group of women was not only providing one another with some much-needed comic relief, they were thinking together—Mindsharing—about issues in their relationships with their children, their partners, their world. A female friend of mine explained that when two women go to a public restroom together to talk, whether it's about husbands, dates, relationships, work, or children, often the other women in the restroom will join in the conversation and offer advice.

Now this may not be big news for at least half of you, but it does show that long before social media or even the Internet was invented, women have been crowdsourcing their relationship questions, dilemmas, and decisions. But why? According to neuropsychiatrist Louann Brizendine, author of *The Female Brain*, the brain centers of women for both language and hearing have 11 percent more neurons than those of men. The hippocampus—the part of the brain that is in charge of emotion and memory formation—is also larger in women than in men. The same is true for the "wiring" in the female brain responsible for language and observing emotions in others.[6] Brizendine also found that when women are communicating they get flooded by a rush of the hormones oxytocin and dopamine. She calls it "the biggest, fattest neurological reward you can get outside of an orgasm."[7]

Again, this may not be news for half of you.

Women are not only great communicators, they have been forming social support groups since humans lived in caves. Evolutionary biology suggests that while "fight or flight" is the male response to stress, "tend and befriend" is the alternate or female response to threat.[8] While the men were out hunting, in order to tend to their offspring and ensure their survival, women sought out social groups for mutual defense. The suggestion is that women are more likely to seek social support in times of stress.

When it comes to relationship stress, women have been talking to one another in the bathroom, at the watercooler, and in more formal support groups, and seeking one another's advice. But unless you have a bathroom that can hold at least 250 women, it's not Mindsharing. It may be gossip. It may be support. It may be wise counsel. But it's not Mindsharing.

Through social media, we all have the power to Mindshare our relationships on a much larger scale (think outside the bathroom). Mindsharing with a large crowd regarding your relationship or love life can yield very different answers from a group of your closest friends. Close friends do not give crowd wisdom. Often our friends want to spare our feelings, help us rationalize our behavior, and fail to give unbiased advice.

The Facebook group I infiltrated was like a group of best friends, only in this case there were tens of thousands of women helping one another out through daily challenges of all types. Mindsharing opens up the door to share our relationship issues and get help in making decisions on a much larger scale than we've seen before.

There is a final footnote to my story of visiting this group. When I shared my experience with my Facebook friends, word got out that a man had infiltrated this women-only group under false pretenses. I made some women quite angry, but I apologized and promised never to set foot (or Facebook profile) again in a group where I did not belong.

I'm not giving the name of the group in this book, but if you ever run across it you'll recognize it by one of its most popular posts:

"Lior Zoref is a moron."

SO MANY QUESTIONS

In our pursuit of meaningful and happy relationships, we all have many questions about this "Crazy Little Thing Called Love."

Mindsharing takes away the guesswork, and we can be wiser than we ever thought possible when we rely on the wisdom of the crowd in matters of the heart.

If a guy like me—awkward and completely bewildered and terrified by the opposite sex—ended up with hundreds of dates, then Mindsharing can do anything. It can help you find the love of your life, turn you into a dating expert, and solve your most complex romantic issues.

But don't just take my word for it, try it yourself. Be honest. Be vulnerable. Be courageous. Step outside your comfort zone, and I promise, the results will amaze you.

And if you still don't believe me, then just ask my mother.

She will give you an earful.

10.

IT TAKES A REALLY BIG VILLAGE
(Mindsharing Your Way to Being a Better Parent)

L et's state the obvious—it's not easy being a parent. Babies don't arrive with an operating manual or a sixty-day trial period with a money-back guarantee. Toddlers don't arrive with a manual either. Or teenagers. Or college-age children who show up on your doorstep and decide to move back home. The bottom line is, as parents, we rarely know what we're doing, and what we don't know seems to only increase as the years go by. Often it seems the best we can hope for is to do better than our parents, who hoped to do better than their parents, and on and on and on.

It's only in the past one hundred years that we have lived in nuclear families. For the 69,900 years before that, we lived as extended families—multiple generations, neighbors, communities living together and sharing the tasks of parenting and raising children. We have all heard the phrase *it takes a village to raise a child*, but truth be told, it also takes a village to raise a parent.

A really big village.

Very few of us have that village in place. While the human race was built on extended families living together in supportive communities or tribes, according to the 2012 census data, multigenerational households make up only 5 percent of all family households, and 37 percent of children in the United States are living in single-parent homes.[1] Overall, for the last few decades the trend in the United States has "been toward smaller households, fewer family and married-couples households, and more people living alone, especially at older ages."[2] There is a void, but Mindsharing has the power to help fill that void.

You may not live in a village, and your extended family may live a great distance away, but when you turn to the crowd you can get help making the tough decisions that used to be decided in family meetings or tribal councils. With Mindsharing, regardless of how many people make up your household or how far away your extended family lives, you don't have to do it alone.

The crowd can't babysit for you. Or help you rock a colicky baby to sleep at night. They can't help you discipline in real time, but their input and value can be just as meaningful. When we don't have a family member to turn to, we can turn to the crowd and get the wisdom of large groups of experienced parents, and the consolation from parents who are going through the same trials and tribulations.

LET ME SHOW YOU A PICTURE

As parents, we proudly show pictures of our children to any captive audience. We boast of their accomplishments. Johnny is walking at eight months. Susie is only two years old and can recite the alphabet—in four different languages. Little Joey is on the honor roll in kindergarten. It's easy to share their successes, because somehow we believe that this must reflect our success as parents. It's harder, however, to share the times when Johnny and Susie and Joey had us at our wit's end. When we were in tears in the aisle of the grocery store with no idea what to do with our little bundle of terror, convinced that whatever we were doing was wrong. I know parents who (only half jokingly) say they are starting a savings account for the day their child goes to therapy.

It takes humility to go to the crowd as parents and ask for help. "Help!" is both a powerful prayer and a quick and easy way to access the wisdom of the crowd. Mindsharing can help you become a better parent, and also show you that there is a crowd of parents who know your pain and have your back.

FINDING YOUR CROWD

BabyCenter.com is one of the largest digital resources for new parents. With more than thirty-six million subscribers globally, it claims to reach one out of every five new parents (mostly moms) online. As such, it is a powerful resource and offers one-stop shopping for Mindsharing your parenting dilemmas. With groups for virtually every topic—fertility, pregnancy, breast-feeding, newborns, toddlers, tweens, and teens—there is no parenting issue you can't Mindshare to solve. There are even "Mommy Mentors" for each trimester of pregnancy. If you can't find your place to Mindshare among the more than eighteen thousand groups—including Teen Moms from Kentucky, Abnormally Stinky Diapers, and Nutty Buddies—you can start your own group. (Keep in mind, however, that "European Sperm Donors" has been taken.)

BabyCenter has many forums that are a great place to practice Mindsharing, but more and more parents are also turning to

Facebook groups. In many ways, this is a more effective and immediate way to Mindshare because you can get alerts instantly and participate in the discussion while you are on Facebook. Since we need parenting wisdom many times during the day, this becomes very convenient. Another important feature is that you can join Facebook parenting groups specific to your city or town, and connect with parents who perhaps shop at the same grocery store with their own "little bundle of terror." Many of these groups are for moms only (dads, don't try to join, trust me on this one), but more are being created for dads as well. Don't see a dad group in your area? Start one. Facebook makes it easy. There are also groups that are values-aligned or specific to a particular parenting strategy or discipline: Attachment Parenting Anonymous, Co-Sleeping Insomniacs, Breastfeeding Vegans, and my favorite, Jewish Moms Talk Mommy Stuff.

From birthday party ideas to discipline woes, the magic of Mindsharing to become a better parent is that you realize you're not in this child-rearing business alone. Raising the future generation is no small matter, but with a like-minded crowd coaching you, the pressure is definitely lessened if not relieved. There is also benefit in knowing that for every mistake and misstep, there is another parent out there who has done the same or worse. When we turn to the crowd, not only do we get wisdom and expert advice, we can get a whole lot of humor. If you worry about overreacting when your child is sick, go to the forum on BabyCenter.com and read the story of one woman named Katherine whose daughter projectile-vomited so violently, the new mom (who had just recently watched *The Exorcist*) not only called the pediatrician—she also called a priest.

Only another parent can understand the deep love and the profound joy that comes with raising a child. And only another parent can understand the intense worry and overwhelming self-doubt that also goes along for the ride. Imagine the job of parenting as tightrope-walking over the Grand Canyon while forty-five-mile-an-hour winds blow.

Mindsharing is your safety net.

PARENTING TIPS FOR MINDSHARING

WHATSAPP. Another useful platform for Mindsharing when it comes to parenting is WhatsApp (www.whatsapp.com). This free, cross-platform, mobile messaging tool is becoming very popular for parents who don't want to share intimate details about their children or their own parenting struggles on social media, but still want the benefits of crowd wisdom from a group of friends. You can create a WhatsApp Mindsharing Group among your friends and intimates and privately share more personal details within this closed platform—and get better answers without the risk of information going public. Whats App also works seamlessly across multiple devices. You can message and respond to the group in real time from your mobile device.

QUORA. Every child is unique, but in many cases the questions we have while raising our kids are very similar. Not every dilemma calls for you to Mindshare a question to Facebook, or BabyCenter, or WhatsApp. As we've discussed, Mindsharing can take time, so before asking a question and engaging your crowd (or a public crowd in a conversation) you should start by searching for an answer to that question. In other words, the question has most likely already been asked, answered, and the crowd wisdom generated. Quora is a great place to search for collective parenting intelligence. And to save even more time (which every parent needs) you can do a Google search for answers in Quora simply by typing in your question and adding "site:quora.com" to the end of your question. This way you will only see results from Quora. If you get no results, then by all means Mindshare for your solutions and you will be helping the next parent who comes along with the same issue.

BE BRIEF. If you do post a question on Facebook or Baby-Center or Quora, make sure it's very brief and to the point. These forums are usually very busy with questions, and many of these questions have too many details. No one wants to hear your life story, or a long conversation about your child (unless they are closely related to you). When asking a question, we must keep it short and simple to understand. The shorter and clearer your question, the more replies you will get. It's as simple as that.

BECAUSE I SAID SO

One day, when my daughter Maya was seven years old, she came home from school crying. I approached her as all fathers approach their crying daughters—with great fear and trepidation. But I was her father, so whatever dragon had made her cry, I was prepared to slay it.

"What's wrong, my Maya?" I asked.

I was prepared for any answer. A boy had pushed her. Another girl hadn't played with her. The teacher was mean. Whatever or whoever had caused my daughter to cry would pay the price. I was Father, hear me roar. I even mentally started writing a strongly worded letter to the principal.

I was tough.

What was the source of my daughter's anguish and despair? Her friend was drinking a Coke at school. Maya isn't allowed to drink Coke. Maya told me she was jealous of her friend. She went on to explain that all of her friends have things she doesn't have, and this makes her jealous and sad.

"It's not fair," she said.

Uh oh. I was in trouble. I couldn't go out and slay a can of Coke or write it a strongly worded letter. And I couldn't allow Maya to drink a Coke just because her friend did or because she was jealous.

I decided to give her my best speech about what's really important in life and what isn't. I explained to her that other people will always have things we don't and vice versa. I explained how some things are not healthy, how advertising agencies and companies hope that we will always want what someone else has. This is how they make money. I then segued into a brilliant discussion of marketing strategy.

Somewhere around the topic of product placement, I lost her. She wasn't having any of it. Life was unfair. I was unfair. She couldn't have a Coke, and she demanded to know why she couldn't and her friend could.

I had no choice. I fell back on the last line of defense for all parents in similar situations. I'm not proud of my words. I had sworn as a father that I would never utter them. But I was out of options. I said those dreaded four words that every parent believes will never come out of their mouth.

"Because I said so."

Later that night, full of shame, I turned to my Facebook friends and asked them how I could teach my daughter not to be envious of her friends. How could I explain to her that material things really didn't matter in life? And more important, I asked them how I could have handled the situation better.

Once again, my crowd didn't let me down. Many told me that instead of trying to explain to her why she isn't allowed to drink Coke, I should just explain why I don't drink Coke and set an example by my own healthy behavior.

The crowd also told me to lighten up a bit. "Let the girl have a Coke every once in a while" was the wisdom of the crowd. They also advised me to never, ever reference product placement, strategic marketing, or advertising agencies while trying to teach my daughter a life lesson.

The next time my daughter feels jealous of one of her friends, I will tell her I understand. I will show empathy. I will speak from my heart, and not my head. And I will turn to the crowd and ask them how they have handled similar situations with their children.

With Mindsharing, there isn't a dragon that I can't slay.

UNFRIENDED

I could share my parenting dilemma about Maya with my Facebook friends because Maya wasn't on Facebook in 2010. This particular crowd may not be the best place to Mindshare your way to being a better parent, because many of our children have a Facebook account. Some of them have even accepted a friend request from their parents. But nothing, and I mean nothing, will get you unfriended by your child faster than sharing an issue about them publicly on Facebook. Especially if they are teenagers.

Take my advice. They may grudgingly agree to be your "friend" on Facebook, but that doesn't mean they actually want to engage with you.

No one wants to be unfriended on social media by their own child. It's painful. Don't tag your children in embarrassing pictures, and don't hijack their posts and conversations. Watch what they are doing and who they are talking to, but maintain a respectful distance. I know one mother who chooses to digitally parent her teenage son. "Dear Son," she writes on his wall, "Please stop chatting on Facebook, and do your homework. Love, Mom." Luckily, her son has a sense of humor, but on more than one occasion he has stated emphatically that "parents should not be allowed on Facebook." This is why many teens are moving to places free from parents such as Whats App, Instagram, and Snapchat.

Save your conversations with your teenagers for the dinner table.

If you need to Mindshare a dilemma about your child or teenager, Quora is a good place to anonymously get advice. Murray turned to Quora when his nineteen-year-old daughter told him she didn't want to go to college, even though she had been accepted to a prestigious school. Murray's response that he was disappointed and thought she was wasting her future had caused his daughter to run off in tears.

Murray received ten detailed answers on Quora when he asked what he should say or do in this situation with his daughter. The unanimous results of this Mindsharing? Murray was advised to respect his daughter in making her adult decisions, and support her in chasing her dreams. School will always be there, the crowd told him, and success is not measured only in diplomas.

Murray followed the wisdom of the crowd and told his daughter he would support her in whatever she decided to do. He even sent her a link to a video about millionaires who had never been to college. Two years after his Quora question, Murray is happy to report that his daughter is in her second year at a prestigious university.

A REALLY BIG VILLAGE

We all wish for wise parents full of loving advice as we parent our own children. Unfortunately, not all of us have parents who are still living or parents who are all that wise. Quora isn't just a source for Mindsharing your parenting decisions—it's also a place to get the parenting advice you may have needed or still need.

I hope that when my three children are older they will be able to reflect back on all the wise advice their father gave them growing up. Meanwhile, I still need to stockpile the wise advice they will someday need. There is a question on Quora that reads, "What Is the Best Advice Your Father Ever Gave You?" Since it has elicited more than eight hundred responses, I find myself perusing it for wisdom. Here are just a few of the gems from the crowd that I hope to someday share with my children:

- Every person you meet in life, even the last wretch on the street, can teach you something.

- You only really own what you can hold under your left arm at a dead run.

- Every person's life has value.

- You don't know what you don't know.

- No matter what you do . . . don't be an idiot. You don't have to know everything. You just have to know how to find it.

The most important bit of wisdom I will share with my children is that in addition to their loving, immediate family, they have a large, connected family that spans the globe and that is always there for them when they need advice. They will have their own crowd. I will also tell them that their parents made many mistakes, and that when they are parents they will make many mistakes as well.

When it comes to parenting, we are all in the same boat. Sometimes the boat sails along smoothly, and sometimes it seems to be sinking faster than we can bail out the water. But we are never in it alone, and our really big village is always along for the ride, ready to help us be better parents.

All we have to do is ask.

11.

PAGING DOCTOR CROWD
(Mindsharing Your Health)

t is no secret to my crowd that I am somewhat of a hypochondriac. Every headache is a brain tumor. Every time my arm falls asleep, it is a heart attack. I can't even begin to count the numerous deadly diseases I have suffered from but never really had. If I find myself giving a speech in front of a large group and I stumble over a word, I immediately think it must be Landau-Kleffner syndrome (characterized by loss of comprehension and expression of verbal language), not nervousness. If I notice a dry patch of skin on my arm, I don't reach for the lotion but immediately look up other symptoms that may corroborate a diagnosis of Refsum disease. On more than one occasion, I have found myself perusing the database of the National Organization for Rare Disorders Web site (it is my secret, shameful wish to someday have a rare disease named after me). But my own hypochondria aside, Mindsharing offers us a rare and unique opportunity to turn to the crowd for decision making about our most important asset in life—our health.

While researching this chapter, I found myself in the middle of a medical mystery. I had a cough. A persistent cough. I didn't have a fever, but I was coughing day and night. Now if I were to search this symptom on any of the popular health Web sites such as WebMD, Healthline, or MedicineNet, I could jump to the conclusion that I had lung cancer or perhaps a fungal infection.

Rather than planning my own funeral, I decided to see my doctor. She ran blood tests and took some X-rays, but found nothing to explain my cough. She referred me to another doctor who was an expert in lung diseases, who (after more tests) discovered nothing and referred me to yet another physician who was an ear, nose, and throat expert. In the end, I saw five different doctors and still had no answers. I was confused, frustrated, and still coughing day and night. I wondered if perhaps this was the first symptom of the illness that would someday be known as the rare Lior Zoref syndrome.

Remembering Deborah's story and how her Facebook crowd was able to diagnose and save her son Leo, I decided to turn to my Facebook friends and see if a little Mindsharing could diagnose my mystery illness. This was my post:

I'm about to start a presentation in a conference at Asuta private hospital. As a hypochondriac, I love these conferences. I feel that I'm in good hands. . . .

I'm waiting to go onstage in a few minutes, and I'm taking the time until I start to get your advice on a private medical issue. In the past few weeks, I've been coughing a lot. I've had X-rays (which didn't show any problem) and blood tests (which showed minor signs of an infection). The doctors gave me antibiotics (Zinat and Roxo), but they're not helping.

No experts can manage to figure out what is causing this troubling cough and I'm curious to see if crowd wisdom will help where my doctors are failing. . . .

So what do you say? I'm sick of coughing. . . .

After only two hours, I received dozens of suggestions from my crowd of five thousand. Now, as I mentioned in the chapter on love, I believe a spreadsheet can solve almost any problem known to man, so I created a spreadsheet to organize the diagnoses I received from the crowd. I divided the suggestions into groups and counted the answers that fell into each category. This was the result:

Whooping Cough	11
Gastroesophageal Reflux Disease	8
Allergies	6
Stress	3
Asthma	2
Virus	1

My crowd had diagnosed me with whooping cough.

The next day I followed up with my primary physician and asked her if this persistent cough could be whooping cough. She said that it was unlikely, since everyone is vaccinated for this disease, but she tested me anyway (I kept insisting and I think she just wanted to get me out of the office). The lab results came back, and the diagnosis was clear. Whooping cough.

I called my doctor, and by this time I was a bit angry. I said, "Why is it that five doctors didn't think it could be whooping cough? How did you miss this?"

She said, "Lior, I have been a physician for thirty years. This is the first time I have ever seen someone with whooping cough."

Once again, Mindsharing had helped me personally and proven itself more powerful than the five experts who had examined me. Now in no way, shape, or form am I telling you to turn your health care over to the crowd entirely. Experts can be wrong. Crowds can be wrong as well. But just as we saw with Deborah's story in the introduction, the crowd wisdom has the power to change our lives when it comes to our medical care. Everyone knows it is a good idea to seek out a second opinion, but with Mindsharing you get not just a second opinion—you get a second opinion based on the intelligence of five hundred or five thousand or fifty thousand. Think of Mindsharing as another tool in your health care toolbox.

SEARCHING *ABOUT* YOUR HEALTH IS NOT MINDSHARING *FOR* YOUR HEALTH

The New York Times reports that four out of five Internet users have searched the Web for health information.[1] We've all done it. But Googling your symptoms, reading health Web sites, and even searching rare disease databases are not Mindsharing. When you do an Internet search of a particular symptom, you will get a biased list of results. This is not crowd wisdom. The results are often skewed toward extreme and even fatal examples, which is why they get a lot of attention, and why these results show up first on Internet searches. The results will often also be biased due to heavy manipulation done by pharmaceutical companies. There is credible medical information on the Internet, but to get to it you have to navigate through a lot of speculation, anecdotes, and advertising. Health care is big money, and where there is big money, there is often big manipulation. The bottom line is it's very hard to know if the source you're looking at is credible (unless you are a medical professional).

Mindsharing solves this problem, especially if you describe

symptoms to a crowd and ask for their advice based on their experience. You can ask a doctor for advice, but a doctor will always advise you based on his or her research, education, and clinical experience with a limited pool of patients. But when you're polling a big crowd for their experience as patients, you tap into a whole other pool of equally useful knowledge that is far more likely to be unbiased.

Mindsharing doesn't replace seeing your physician, but it is an additional health resource that is readily available. You can go to your doctor, as I did with my whooping cough, and share the results of your Mindsharing with him. Hopefully, he will seriously consider your crowd-based "second opinion." Mindsharing is also a great tool to help you find a doctor or specialist. It's a great way to get independent recommendations for any medical professional. For example, perhaps you ask your crowd for the best pediatrician for your child. Depending on the size and diversity of your crowd, you may want to specify within a certain geographic location or that you are looking for someone who specializes in childhood diabetes or ADHD. Whatever the case, the more specific you are, the more relevant the recommendations. The person whose name comes up the most, or whose name has the most likes, represents the wisdom of the crowd for this particular question. Of course, you still need to meet this doctor yourself, or perhaps the top three the crowd has recommended, but Mindsharing will have saved you the time spent researching pediatricians on your own or prevented you from getting biased results from a general Internet search.

There's a lot the crowd can do to support you in your health care, and there's a lot they can't do. The crowd can't do a physical examination. It can't prescribe medication or see you in its office.

What the crowd can do for you is support you in making the best health care decisions possible. We can use Mindsharing to get a second opinion, understand medical treatments and alternative options, and understand our own health just a little bit better. In an era when medical professionals seem to have less and less time to listen to our concerns, it's comforting to know there is a crowd out there to talk to, and who will listen.

DISRUPTING THE DOCTORS

I was waiting to take my turn onstage to speak to a crowd of hepatologists—physicians who are experts in the liver—about Mindsharing. As I waited, I listened to a distinguished professor who was also chairman of the Liver Association speak. She was presenting eleven test cases involving liver disease. Each hepatologist in the audience had a remote control so they could respond in real time and choose the best treatment out of four possible options.

Naturally, I was intrigued. Here we had a group of expert medical professionals. I expected that approximately 85 percent of the doctors would choose the same treatment out of the four options. The first case was presented and the answers from the audience submitted. It was almost an even four-way split among the professionals. I thought this was just a fluke. But for each of the next ten cases presented, the opinions on the best treatment were also divided equally among the four choices.

I was curious about these results, and grateful that I wasn't at that moment a liver patient trying to choose a treatment option.

I am not in any way suggesting that nonexperts would have more knowledge than the liver experts and be able to choose the best treatment, but I am reminded how difficult it can be as patients to navigate health care and health options. This is where I believe the crowd can come in with valuable expertise. If the audience at that talk had consisted of liver patients, I believe their answers (based on their personal experience) might not have been so evenly divided. I also believe that instead of just fifty doctors, an audience of fifty thousand doctors would have provided a definitive best treatment option out of the four choices. Mindsharing among a large crowd of experts is a powerful practice, and we see the benefits in LinkedIn groups (as we've discussed) and other specialized social networks for professionals who are experts in their field.

If I need surgery, I'm not going to ask the crowd to perform my surgery. But I would ask the crowd about my best options, and benefit from their collective experience. I would also ask a large crowd of experts to get my collective second opinion.

When I present the subject of crowd wisdom to doctors, it's not easy. As experts, they often find it difficult to understand how a big crowd of nonexperts can generate wisdom. They also no doubt feel threatened. They've invested a lot of time and money in becoming experts, and of course, when medical decisions go wrong, there are real life-and-death consequences. But there's also no doubt that Mindsharing is a disruptive force in the medical world. The crowd isn't going away, and while it can never replace physicians and their invaluable knowledge and experience, Mindsharing is holding medical experts to a higher standard of accountability and transparency.

Mindsharing has the potential to affect every area of our health care. Medical information, expertise, and the experience of others is now open-source information. We don't experience medical difficulties or medical successes in silence or isolation. Here are just a few ways Mindsharing is helping us all when it comes to our health.

ADVANCING MEDICINE. Treato (www.treato.com) is a company that is harnessing the collective wisdom of billions of health conversations online and indexing what they call the "Social Health Web." By monitoring all public information about pharmaceuticals from blogs, forums, social networks, and the like, they are systematically finding new uses for existing drugs based on the wisdom and experience of the people who are actually taking these pharmaceuticals.

While the Treato user interface will probably change over time, currently when you go to its Web site you see a search bar entitled "See what millions of patients are saying." The rest is simple. You enter the name of a medication and press "Search." You then get a short description of the medication and a list of top concerns and detailed positive and negative reviews. If you're concerned about a specific side effect, you can add that to your initial search. For example, I can search "Lipitor and muscle pain" and get data and a list of what other people are experiencing with that particular side effect. If nothing comes up, then I might have to look elsewhere for the source of my muscle pain.

What's unique about Treato is that it's tapping into the real expert wisdom—the people who are actually taking the drugs prescribed to them—not the wisdom of the drug's manufacturer.

Treato is mining the Internet for users who have posted their experiences with a particular drug or treatment—perhaps on a blog or a Web site. They then use an algorithm to find a common signal from among these users. Gideon Mantel, the founder of Treato, told me that after reviewing all the data the site has collected, they have found many surprising cases. For example, many women have reported two popular cough syrups, Mucinex and Robitussin, as not only relieving their cough but also helping them to get pregnant. In this case, their algorithm found three hundred to four hundred women who wrote on their blog about a possible connection between taking these medications and getting pregnant. As 3 to 4 percent of Internet users share health-related experiences,[2] this means that there are potentially ten thousand similar experiences among women. This sends a clear signal for the pharmaceutical industry to do research investigating this new potential medical use.

Finding a clear signal sometimes can come from somewhere else—from silence. The FDA recently approved two weight-loss drugs (after considering them for ten years)—Belviq and Qsymia. Weight loss is a very popular topic, and one might expect to see many posts and conversations about these drugs. Treato found a surprisingly low number of posts about them. This lack of signal is actually a very important signal. It means that at this moment, patients don't see real value in these particular weight-loss drugs.

Now, I'm not recommending cough medicine over a fertility expert, and it will take time and thorough clinical testing to confirm or refute the anecdotal experiences of patients taking any drug, but crowd wisdom can't be discounted. Mantel says Treato has found another fifteen thousand cases of suspected new uses for existing drugs, what doctors call "off-label" use. Who knows what the crowd might discover? If a cough syrup might save you thousands on fertility treatments, perhaps the crowd can help cure some of our most perplexing medical and health issues.

ADVANCING DIAGNOSIS. Sometimes we can Mindshare our way to health without even trying. In 2012, a young man decided to use a home-pregnancy test that his ex-girlfriend had left behind in his apartment. To his surprise, after he took the home test, it came back positive. Not believing that he was the first man ever to get pregnant, he just chalked it up to the unreliability of home pregnancy tests. He told his friend about what happened and they joked about posting online that he was pregnant.[3]

They ended up sharing the story on Reddit, thinking it would get a few laughs. Now if you are not familiar with Reddit, it is a social news and entertainment Web site. People use Reddit to share and rate interesting stories. Instead of pressing a "like" button as in Facebook, Reddit users (called Redditors) have up and down buttons for each story. Based on these buttons, users collectively decide which stories are most interesting based on the up votes or down votes. In a sense, Reddit is a Mindsharing platform for finding the most interesting news and entertainment stories.

After sharing the pregnancy joke on Reddit, the two received more than 1,500 responses. Many of them said that a positive pregnancy test in a male is a sign of testicular cancer. The young man immediately went to see his doctor, who found a small tumor on his testicle. Luckily, because of the wisdom of the crowd, the cancer was discovered at an early stage and treatment was both possible and effective.

The two hadn't gone looking for crowd wisdom, but were lucky enough to stumble upon it anyway.

ADVANCING SCIENCE. Mindsharing in the area of health has profound implications not only for us individually, but for the scientific community at large. Tapping into the power of the crowd to find cures for diseases is already happening—with astounding results. For more than ten years, an international team of experts has been trying to unlock the structure of AIDS-related enzymes called Mason-Pfizer proteases, with no success. We have trillions of cells in our body, and inside each cell are proteins consisting of long chains of amino acids that tell the cell what to do. There are thousands of different types of proteins consisting of one hundred to one thousand different amino acids. Each protein folds up into a very specific (and complicated) shape. This shape determines the function of the protein. When you can decode the structure of a protein, you can understand how it works and also specifically target it to react to certain drugs. Figuring out the best structure of a protein is one of the most difficult tasks in biology. It takes a lot of time, a lot of money, and in the case mentioned above, even befuddles computers. Why? Because the number of different ways even a small protein can fold is astronomical. Then some students from the University of Washington came up with a unique idea to create a collaborative online game that allows players to manipulate or "fold" proteins. Their belief was that humans are better at solving puzzles than computers, so they created the game Foldit.

Within ten days, a team of twenty-five players (among the 236,000 players on Foldit) had solved the molecular puzzle and advanced the search for a cure for AIDS. Zoran Popović, director of the University of Washington's Center for Game Science, said in a press release that Foldit shows that together novices can become experts, "capable of producing first-class scientific discoveries." Perhaps this is just the beginning of a new scientific collaboration between citizens and experts that will use Mindsharing to solve our most troubling health concerns globally.

WE INTERRUPT THE WORLD OF MEDICINE TO BRING YOU THE FOLLOWING IMPORTANT MESSAGE

Many would say that the medical community (and health care in general) needs a major disruption. New doctors in the United States are trained to spend an average of eight minutes face-to-face with patients. Eight minutes. Hardly enough time to introduce yourself, much less give a thorough explanation of your health problems and ask questions. Hardly enough time to get answers. Is it any wonder that 1.4 billion searches a month on Google are health related? Seeing a physician has turned into a form of speed dating.

Perhaps this is one reason why more and more people are turning to the crowd for medical wisdom. CrowdMed (www .crowdmed.com) is one site that is looking to the future of medicine as more and more reliant on, and supplemented by, the wisdom of the crowd. Founder Jared Heyman started Crowd-Med after his younger sister, Carly, spent three years suffering from an undiagnosed illness.

In 2003, Carly started experiencing strange medical symptoms. She slept fourteen hours a night but was still tired during the day. She was experiencing hot flashes, night sweats, anxiety, and unexplained weight loss. Carly was only seventeen years old. She dropped out of school and her family thought she might be suffering from depression.

Over the course of three years, Carly saw two dozen different doctors. Each specialist would treat the symptoms the best they could, but no one could determine a diagnosis. Her family had more than $100,000 in medical bills but no answers. Eventually, she received the opportunity to consult with a team of interdisciplinary experts at the National Institutes of Health. After a week of tests, they came back with a diagnosis—fragile X-associated primary ovarian insufficiency (FXPOI). It affects just one in fifteen thousand females. After three weeks of treatment most of the symptoms disappeared.

Her experience, and the ultimate solving of her medical mystery by a "team" at NIH, was Jared Heyman's motivation and inspiration. He used her experience as the first test case for the more than four thousand registered MDs (in this case, medical detectives) on CrowdMed. Her case was solved in just three days, not three years. Her own doctors had never heard of FXPOI. This is not surprising. There are more than seven thousand rare diseases in the world—what single physician could possibly keep track of all of this medical information? (For an updated list of Mindsharing resources for health, including a video of a conversation with CrowdMed founder Jared Heyman, please visit mindsharing.info/health.)

CrowdMed is trying to solve the world's most challenging cases—cases that doctors are failing to diagnose—through a crowd wisdom methodology called "prediction markets."

Prediction markets are a methodology for making predictions based on the wisdom of the crowd. The crowd is being challenged to make a prediction and associate it with a probability. Each person gives his bet price (it could be a virtual number), which relates to the sense of confidence in his prediction. At the end of the process, using this methodology, you are looking for the highest accumulated bet on a single prediction, which is then chosen as the prediction with the highest probability of coming true. Prediction markets are used for sales forecasting and to predict a new product's success in the market—and in this case, for medical diagnosis. CrowdMed gives a probability based on the crowd's wisdom as to which diagnosis is most likely.

With CrowdMed, patients save time and money and, more important, get a list of the most likely diagnostic outcomes for their medical issue. After submitting your case to CrowdMed, you can go to your doctor with the possibility the crowd has determined to be the most likely solution to your problem. CrowdMed also helps patients make the best use of the eight minutes spent with their doctor. Mindsharing is proving to be the disruption that the medical community needs.

WASH YOUR HANDS

Professor Gabriel Barabash is the CEO of one of the leading hospitals in Israel, Tel Aviv Sourasky Medical Center. We were in the middle of an interesting discussion about Mindsharing and the future of health care when he suggested we do an experiment. He told me that one of the biggest challenges in hospitals around the world was hospital-acquired infections. These infections cause 100,000 deaths each year in the United States alone and are transmitted mostly by hospital staff who fail to regularly wash their hands.

We decided to see how a crowd of nonexperts might solve this problem in hospitals and compare it with the solution from a crowd of experts. We made a list of the platforms for Mindsharing this experiment with nonexperts (Facebook) and also found a LinkedIn group made up of 120,000 experts— Healthcare Executives Network. Overall, we published the question on fifteen different platforms including Facebook,

LinkedIn, Quora, TED Conversations, and other targeted Q&A sites.

We posted this question:

I need your help.

My name is Gabi Barabash and I am the CEO of a large university-affiliated medical Center in Tel Aviv, Israel. Hospital-acquired infections are causing 100,000 deaths each year in the US and many more worldwide. This is one of the biggest challenges in hospitals today. Much of the blame rests on us, the hospital staff, since these infections are transmitted far more often when hospital personnel fail to regularly wash their hands and practice proper hygiene.

Hand washing is the single most important measure for reducing the risks of transmitting infections. Yet, the harsh reality is that too many physicians and nurses, including those in the most advanced medical centers, do not bother to wash their hands regularly even though an antiseptic gel is accessible close to each patient's bedside.

Disciplinary measures are difficult to enforce because it is impossible to document each patient contact. An alternative solution based on electronic systems (with RFID tags) is too expensive and complicated to implement throughout a large institution.

This is why I need your help. I am looking for creative ideas to solve this problem.

Try to think of an idea that can make a behavioral change among the medical staff so that they will routinely wash their hands before as well as after examining a patient.

I look forward to receiving your ideas. One simple idea can help save many lives.

In the days that followed our posting, we received 318 valid ideas—93 from experts and 225 from nonexperts. We looked carefully into each and every idea. We grouped the ideas into different categories such as training for medical personnel, public awareness campaigns for patients, punishments, rewards, and many more. We counted the number of ideas that fell into each category. There was one suggestion that surprised us. Hospital soaps have an antiseptic smell to them, and the suggestion was to use soaps with different and more pleasant scents in order to encourage people to use them. It was a great idea.

What we discovered was that the crowd of nonexperts had exactly the same priorities as the medical professionals. The first priority for both was educating the medical professionals, and the second priority was educating patients as they indirectly influence the staff.

While this didn't immediately save a hundred thousand lives, it did show that ordinary people can understand medical challenges and come up with the same results as experts. It is yet one more example of a paradigm shift that is happening when it comes to our health. Experts have wisdom. Nonexperts have collective wisdom. Just as we saw with Foldit and CrowdMed, the potential for solving health challenges is that much greater when we work together to mine the collective wisdom for gold.

IMAGINE THE POSSIBILITIES

My mother-in-law, Sara, was a truly amazing woman. Six years ago, she was diagnosed with cancer. The doctors gave her the best treatment possible at the time, but after a year of her

undergoing treatment, they came back and gave us the horri-
ble news. It wasn't working. They said the only hope was for us
to choose among three different experimental treatments.

We didn't have a clue about which treatment to choose. We
cried a lot. Finally, we decided on one option, and did the only
thing left to do. We prayed.

Unfortunately, this beautiful woman, my children's grand-
mother, died two months later.

For four years I have asked myself if there wasn't something
else we could have done. Something. Anything. Could we have
done something to save her life?

In 2011, Nature.com published a research study about a
crowdsourced platform for patients called PatientsLikeMe
.com. The site is an online community of patients who are recording and sharing their medical data. They report their
blood tests, the medications they take, their symptoms, and
how they are feeling. Hundreds of thousands of patients openly
share their medical information to help other patients make
medical decisions.

The patients aren't paid. It is simply one patient helping another through the collective wisdom of thousands.

I know if my mother-in-law were alive today, I would be using
this site to search for the optimal treatment for her. If I had
known about the site, we would have had a place to go to explore the three different treatments and would have heard
from real people just like her who had faced the same choices.
Maybe what would have saved her was not better medicine or
better doctors, but better wisdom.

I challenge all of you to look at your health care with new
eyes. There is wisdom out there that can complement the wisdom
of any expert. It is saving lives in countless ways. Solving medical
mysteries. Finding possible cures for diseases we thought were

incurable. The future of Mindsharing when it comes to our health is a future with incredible possibility.

I dedicate this chapter to Sara, and to the countless others whose lives may have been saved by the wisdom of the crowd. I am reminded once again that together we are so much stronger than we are alone. It gives me hope.

HOW TO MINDSHARE YOUR DREAMS INTO REALITY

12.

I HAVE A DREAM
(The Power of Crowd Dreaming)

It all started with a midlife crisis.

It was the summer of 2008 and I had just celebrated my thirty-eighth birthday. Life was exactly as it should be. I had a successful career at Microsoft, an incredible wife, Ayala, and two amazing children, Maya and Ori. Life was comfortable and my daily routine was spent balancing a demanding career in the high-tech industry with the demands of raising two young children and spending time with my family. I hadn't had a life full of many adventures. I had gone to work for Microsoft immediately after graduating as a computer science engineer. Technically, I was still in my first full-time job. Was this it? Had I made all my big life choices already, and was there nothing left to do, to accomplish, or to reach for?

Then I started thinking about turning forty. If you have just turned thirty-eight, take my advice and don't start ruminating about turning forty. Or do. It depends on just how quickly you wish to completely upend your comfortable life. On that day, I started thinking how far I had come from that scared, awkward boy who spent his days alone in his room. And then I started in with the questioning. Had I achieved everything I wanted to achieve before I turned forty? What was left for me? What was still ahead for me in the second part of my life?

I have heard it said that to be happy you have to have someone to love, something to do, and something to look forward to. I had someone to love and something to do—but what did I have to look forward to? What were my dreams?

I thought about an old dream I had of getting a PhD and felt my heart begin to beat faster. This is my sure sign that whatever I am thinking about is something I need to do. Some people hear ringing in their ears. Some people begin to sweat. For me, a rapid heartbeat is a sign to pay attention.

What do you secretly dream about that makes your heart beat so loud and so fast you simply can't ignore it?

It took me two years of thinking about this dream, talking it over with my wife, friends, and colleagues before I decided to retire from Microsoft and begin pursuit of my PhD in education, with an emphasis and dissertation on crowd wisdom. All of this happened in time for my fortieth birthday. My midlife crisis was complete.

All of this happened at the same time I heard about the first TEDx event in Israel. TEDx events were launched in 2009 as a way for local areas to have a self-organized, TED-like experience. The moment I heard about it, I knew I had to attend and listen to all the speakers in Tel Aviv with ideas worth spreading.

How did I know? Rapid heartbeat strikes again. I was determined to attend.

Thousands of people applied to get tickets to an event that could hold only hundreds. I knew I had to be proactive and creative if I wanted to get a seat. At the time, my good friend Yosi Taguri and I had a video blog covering technology news and events. I decided to contact one of the organizers and offer to cover the event in our video blog. To my amazement, they accepted, and Yosi and I were on our way to TEDx Tel Aviv.

It was an inspiring event. Each speaker presented his or her ideas in eighteen minutes or less. I was moved. I was inspired. It was a full day of my heart beating quickly and loudly, and I felt myself wishing and dreaming that one day I would speak at TEDx. And maybe not just TEDx, but TED. I saw myself, in five or ten years, stepping onto the big TED stage. It was a crazy dream, but maybe, I thought, after I had my PhD, I would be able to share my studies and my ideas with the world.

During the break, Yosi and I recorded a new episode for our video blog, and in a spontaneous moment, I suddenly told my friend about my dream. I should point out that I never shared my dreams with anyone, much less in public. I'm not sure I even had big dreams before that moment. Growing up, I wanted to have friends, then I wanted to get into college, then I wanted to find a woman who might actually want to marry me, and I wanted to have children. I wanted to have a good career and support my family. All of this was practical, what I was raised to accomplish. But I don't think I ever had big, wild dreams of do- ing amazing things. As Yosi and I began recording from TEDx I was so inspired, so full of possibility and hope that I felt I could do anything. And what I most dreamed of doing was pre- senting the power of Mindsharing on the TED stage.

I hesitated for a moment—if you've ever shared a dream with a friend or a family member, you know this hesitation. It's a scary moment, like when you're standing on the top of a high dive, wanting to jump but scared to death. Time seemed to slow down, and in the seconds before I blurted out my dream to Yosi, on camera, I thought, *He is going to think I'm crazy, he is go- ing to laugh at me, and I will regret this forever.*

I jumped anyway.

"Yosi, I have a dream. My dream is to speak at TED. Not in the next year or two, but when I do it, I'll show this video of us when we were young and this dream was born." (You can Google "Lior Zoref I have a dream" and see this video.)

Yosi laughed, and then he got angry. He stopped me and shouted, "There's no chance that someone will give you a chance to be on the TED stage! There's a better chance of you winning the lottery than speaking at TED."

I was deeply hurt and disappointed. I tried to smile at Yosi and at the camera, but couldn't manage to do so. I went back home and tried to forget the incident and forget the dream. I realized Yosi was probably right; I'm just starting my PhD and have a long way to go. I'm not famous. I haven't published anything significant. I probably do have a better chance of winning the lottery than speaking at TED.

A few days later, this episode of our video blog was published and everyone who watched it also saw my confession of my secret dream to speak at TED. My friends saw it. My family saw it. And many people I didn't know also saw it. I felt embarrassed and slightly ashamed of being caught up in the moment. It was my first experience sharing a dream aloud, and I was full of regret.

Then something amazing happened that took me by complete surprise. My social network, my crowd, rallied behind me. Collectively they told me, "Lior, we know you. We think this is a great dream and that you are worthy of speaking at TED. We're going to help you do it."

My crowd decided to make my dream come true.

Almost daily, someone would write to me privately or on my Facebook wall and remind me about my dream or offer advice about how to make it happen. It was a strange situation. I couldn't dismiss or forget about my dream because I was surrounded by a crowd of people who said I should go for it, and who wanted to help.

A few weeks later, one of my Facebook friends, someone I'd

met only once in my life, posted a link on my wall to TED's first ever auditions for new speakers. Her name was Maya Elhalal-Levavi, and she followed the link with these words: "Lior, this is the chance you've been waiting for!"

I was puzzled. Why was this woman I barely knew supporting me in this crazy dream more than my close friend Yosi? It goes back to the power of weak ties that I mentioned in the introduction. Our weak ties are our bridges to new information, new groups, and new experiences. What I've come to learn is that our social network friends, most of whom are our weak ties, have value that is indispensable. Our close friends and family may love us, but that love, and that comfort with who we are and our role in their lives, can often prevent them from seeing our possibility for change, or from seeing us take on a new identity or role in the world. The crowd doesn't operate within the limitations of love. They see only our possibility.

Maya saw my possibility, and in doing so, she helped me to see it as well. I opened the link she provided and read all the details about auditioning for TED.

They were holding auditions in New York City, and anyone who was interested only needed to record a one-minute video of their Big Idea and submit it for review.

Now, I've never auditioned for anything, and it was too soon to go after my dream, and I only had two weeks to make a video, and how could I summarize my ideas in one minute, and it was Passover and most people were on vacation, and I had no idea how to make such a video.

In short, I had a million reasons not to pursue my dream, and a million fears to go along with each reason.

I had only one reason to pursue this dream.

My crowd.

If they believed in me, then I had to believe in me.

I published a status update on Facebook asking if someone had an auditorium where I could record a video. This was the test. If no one did, then it wasn't meant to be and I would try again in the next decade or so.

Someone offered to help me out, and we arranged to meet and record my video audition.

It was a holiday and the kids were out of school. My wife supported my dream and told me to go and record all the videos I wanted, as long as I took my three-year-old son, Ori, with me.

Now, I had another obstacle to overcome. Ori is a gadget fan, a small geek-in-training like his dad, and I knew there was no way he would let me set up a video camera and not want to touch it, take it apart, and put it back together again.

When we are parents and we have dreams, we need to get creative. I took Ori's favorite snack with me to the video shoot. If I gave him the bag, this would give me exactly ten minutes of quiet to record my video.

I hoped it would be enough.

After a few false starts and awful takes, I shared my idea about presenting the first-ever crowdsourced TED talk to be created with the help of my Facebook and Twitter friends. It would be a talk about crowdsourcing created by the crowd. Genius.

Luckily, I finished this last take just as Ori finished his snack.

I submitted the video with the application form and tried to put the whole thing out of my mind and get back to my daily routine. I was scared and feeling vulnerable and insecure. I was sure they would turn me down, and I knew I would feel ashamed for even trying to reach so high. Who was I to dream so big?

A few weeks later, as I was having dinner with some close friends, I opened my smart phone and saw an e-mail from TED. My heart started beating crazily again, and I quickly stepped outside so I could read it in private and deal with my disappointment in private.

I read the first line twice before it sank in.

Congratulations on being selected.

I needed to be in New York in less than two weeks to be part of a special audition they were holding. I was another huge step closer to my dream of being on the TED stage.

I went back into the house and told my wife and friends, "You won't believe the e-mail I just received from TED."

I looked at my wife. She was smiling, but also holding her belly. She was nine months pregnant with our third child. There was no way I could go to New York. She could go into labor any day.

My sweet and wonderful wife took a deep breath and said, "Lior, this is your dream. Go do it, but do it quick. Get on a plane to New York City, audition, then get on a plane home. The baby and I will wait for you." I tried to argue that it wasn't responsible and there's no way she could wait to go into labor (some things you can't control), but she insisted I follow my dream.

This is but one of the many reasons why I love her.

I also knew I had to share this news with my crowd of friends and followers on my blog, and on Facebook and Twitter. Their response and support was also amazing. They had made this happen, and they let me know they were behind me every step of the way. It was a stressful time leading up to the audition. I was nervous about my presentation, worried that my wife was going to go into labor. I almost canceled my flight due to her having contractions (which she insisted she was able to halt after an Internet search told her to drink lots of water).

I boarded my flight more frightened than I've ever been in my life. I didn't want to miss the birth of my child, I didn't know how I would do in my first audition, and there was the very real possibility that either I would fail spectacularly or my dream would come true.

Both options were equally terrifying.

My plane landed and I went immediately to the audition. There were about two hundred people in a beautiful ballroom, and while the audience felt warm and supportive, it was incredibly intimidating.

I planned to begin my audition with a funny story, and I told myself that if the audience laughed, I would stay on the stage, and if they didn't laugh, I would run off the stage and head immediately to the airport. Finally, they introduced me, and with sweat pouring down my face, and my voice shaky, I began.

"I am so excited to be here. But not just because of the audition . . . My wife and I are about to have a baby, any day, maybe even right now. She insisted that I take an eleven-hour flight from Tel Aviv to be here for a few hours to pursue my dream. If I succeed here today, we might even name our new baby TED."

The audience laughed, so I stayed on the stage and began to share my ideas about Mindsharing. I asked the audience to use Twitter and send suggestions for a closing sentence for my talk. I had a friend, Eran Gefen, sitting in the audience with an iPad reviewing the suggestions as they came in. His role was to Mindshare and mine the suggestions for gold. At the end of my audition, he handed me the iPad with my closing sentence (submitted by Aya Shapir). I took another deep breath and finished my audition.

"Great minds think alike, clever minds think together."

I rushed back to the airport, flew home, and a few days later my wife gave birth to our third child.

We named him Assaf Ted Zoref.

(To read the full story of my TED experience, please visit mindsharing.info/ted.)

THE CROWD DREAMS WITH YOU

When I received the formal invitation to speak at TED 2012 in Long Beach, California, I was happy to share the news with my crowd. This wasn't just *my* dream, it was *our* dream. I had only a few months to prepare the talk of my life, and the response from my crowd was overwhelming. Thousands of people congratulated me and said they'd be willing to help. The message was loud and clear.

I wasn't in this alone.

The crowd had motivated me to pursue my dream, and now they were motivating me in a completely new way. My strong ties and my weak ties all came together and cheered me on. Imagine walking through life with a crowd following you around, applauding and encouraging you with every step you take. This is what it felt like.

It's a great feeling. The crowd motivated me to step outside my comfort zone and walk through my fears. It held me up when fear and self-doubt threatened to derail me. This is the ultimate form of Mindsharing. I call it Crowd Dreaming. There is no limit to what you can accomplish when you trust and allow the crowd to dream with you.

I began preparing for my TED talk with nothing. Absolutely nothing. I had a blank PowerPoint presentation and one idea— we can upgrade our thinking and our lives when we harness the power of the crowd. That's it. Hardly enough to fill twelve minutes of stage time.

I needed to turn this idea into a complete talk, and I needed powerful stories to tell. But how would I select the best stories? What would be my main message? How could I visually and viscerally demonstrate the power we have when we tap into the crowd? I had so many questions, and no idea how or where to begin.

So I began to walk my talk. I went to the crowd. I wrote my first blog post where I shared my excitement and my fears, and invited anyone and everyone to join me in creating the first-ever crowdsourced TED talk. I shared this blog post on all my social networks. As I mentioned earlier, one of the first questions I asked was about how best to explain and show crowd wisdom. I mined the collective wisdom for gold, and found the ox idea. It was a brilliant idea, and it was the first time I used Mindsharing to find a creative idea. My crowd had delivered, and now I had to meet the challenge and deliver.

I had to deliver an ox, to be exact.

I shared with you the story of asking for the ox in the introduction, and how crazy I thought it was at first. The crowd gave me confidence and encouragement, and that's what helped me make such a bold move that I was secretly afraid would get me kicked out of TED altogether.

Many people call Israel "The Start-up Nation." There are so many creative people and the start-up scene is very full and busy. When I meet entrepreneurs I always ask them, what is the number one attribute of a successful start-up or a successful business? They always say audacity, or what we call in Hebrew *chutzpah*. When you have chutzpah, you often overstep the bounds of accepted behavior in pursuit of a larger goal. It is why I wanted to jump in on the conversation the girls were having in the ice cream shop, and why my crowd was so insistent I ask for the ox. Chutzpah is courage that opens people's hearts and minds to new ideas.

I continued to Mindshare and create every aspect of my talk with the crowd: interesting stories, the design for my PowerPoint presentation, right down to the picture of me TED would use at the conference. This is how I got the idea to include the faces of the crowd who had helped this dream come true along with my face. It wasn't my creative brilliance that created this poster, but the brilliance of the crowd (which was photographed by a member of my crowd, Meir Pinto).

It was not only a great and creative idea, it was also a way to acknowledge and thank my crowd for encouraging and coaching me along the way. It was an important way to manage my digital relationships and show my appreciation.

The crowd also watched YouTube videos as I rehearsed and gave me feedback and constructive criticism on my stage presence, my way of speaking, and my ability to hold the audience and be interesting. It was an intense process. My fears and my weaknesses were on full display, but this is what made it even more powerful.

When the time came to travel to Long Beach, I was pale and it felt a bit as if I were playing a part in a movie. Was this all real? Had the crowd and I really made my dream come true so quickly? Was it possible? Was the crowd wisdom I was studying and researching more powerful than I had even realized?

Two seasoned TED speakers came up to me and saw how nervous I was. My nervousness was hard to miss. All of Long Beach could hear my teeth chattering. Both the man and the woman wanted to help me out. The man said to me, "Lior, I know exactly how you feel."

"Do you? I'd love to hear," I replied.

"You feel as if you're inside a cannon and someone is going to fire it soon."

"You're absolutely right," I answered. This was exactly how I felt.

Then the woman said to me, "Lior, *I* know exactly how you feel."

"How?" I answered, anxious to see if she would also use the cannon metaphor.

"You are feeling as if you're going to have the best orgasm of your life!"

Every night in Long Beach, before I went to sleep, I took the time to read all the messages from the crowd who had participated and followed me on this journey. I had already made it to TED, but they were still by my side and still encouraging me to finish strong.

> Lior, as the clock is ticking towards your presentation and the familiar faces of your crowd are fading, I hope that you know that you're not alone. You have a noble crowd of people who are proud of being part of the journey you have made. I'm sure that I say this in the name of everyone as I wish you good luck. Have fun. This is your moment. May the force be with you.

Okay, many in my crowd are *Star Wars* fans. Don't judge.

Another post reminded me of just how connected I was to my crowd.

> One of the insights I have in the last few days about crowd wisdom is that it's much more than wisdom. It's also about common fate, something that brings us all together. I feel it as I get the chills and I am so excited to read your experiences at TED. I have goosebumps! Good luck.

And yet another one helped me walk onto the TED stage feeling less alone than I have ever felt in my life.

> The fact that you're having a dream is amazing, but the fact that you're sharing while you make your dream come true is a rare inspiration! Keep on sharing with us because this is what your crowd needs. Thank you.

At the time of writing this book, we're still waiting for TED to publish my talk. I hope that you will be able to see it; me in all my nervous glory, and the crowd right there with me. When the crowd dreams with you, you take the crowd wherever you go. Across continents and time zones, the crowd is always there. Your success is their success, and their inspiration is your inspiration. It is a powerful testament to just how connected we are and just how easy it is to tap into that connection when we Mindshare our dreams.

When you are passionate about a dream, or a life choice, or a new career, the crowd will see your passion and become passionate themselves. Meaningful connections don't just happen with our closest family and friends, they can happen through the most distant of ties. Our crowd is more invested in our future than in our past, and this makes any dream possible. As I said earlier, often the people we are closest to can be blinded by who we are, and unable to see who we can become. The crowd can see our potential, so they are often better able to dream with us. Crowd dreaming is about being vulnerable and honest. It's standing at the top of that high dive, taking a deep breath, being afraid, and jumping anyway.

What is your secret dream? What epic thing do you want to do that makes your heart beat fast and your voice get shaky? What do you imagine for your life? Now take all those fears, those doubts, those reasons why it couldn't, shouldn't, wouldn't happen and hand them to your crowd.

If you're standing on that high dive, just take a leap of faith and jump. Make it a glorious swan dive or an inglorious belly flop, it doesn't matter. The crowd is there with you to cheer you on. And when you fail, as we all inevitably do at times, the crowd is there to comfort you, motivate you, and help you get back on your feet. And when the crowd is with you, any dream is possible.

This chapter is the story of how the crowd helped me make my dream come true. In the next chapter we will look at how you can discover what your dream is, and exactly how you can Mindsharc your way to making it a reality.

13.

SWEET DREAMS

(Mindsharing Your Way to a Successful Life Dream)

When life settled down (a bit) after my adventures on the TED stage, I found myself interested in the secret ingredients for crafting a good dream. At first, I looked for research. And while I found endless research into the dreams we have while we are asleep, I found next to nothing about the dreams we have while we are awake.

Of course, I did what I always do when a search engine, even an academic search engine that results in thousands of research papers, leaves me wanting—I went to my crowd. I asked them, "How would you define a dream? What are the secret ingredients of a good life dream?"

The crowd gave me these answers:

- A life dream is a specific, challenging goal that you aspire to achieve in the future.

- A life dream must be specific and well defined. Being happy or having a successful career is not specific enough.

- A good life dream should be very easy to measure. You have to know when it's accomplished.

- It should be challenging and hard to achieve. A good dream has to seem a bit crazy.

- It should give value to others, as well as to you. It's where your talent meets the needs of the world around you.

- It should make you both inspired and scared. It's something out of your comfort zone but with deep roots in your passion and talent.

- When you think about making your dream come true, you should feel a sense of deep happiness and great achievement.

- It should be your dream and not someone else's. It's not what others expect of you but what you expect of yourself.

My crowd is a wise crowd. Here's the thing about dreams. They don't go away. Once you hear the whisper of *"Someday I want to . . ."* or *"I wish I could . . ."* the seed has been planted and it just waits for the right time or the right impetus to take root and grow.

What are your dreams? They might feel too big or too crazy or too impossible—but that doesn't mean they aren't there inside you, waiting for the right time to make their presence known.

NO TECHNION FOR YOU

When I was in high school, my dream was to be a student at the Technion, one of the world's top technological universities. I wasn't the best student, nor did I have the best grades. But what I did have was a dream. One day, as I was sitting in class, I decided to confess my dream to a guest teacher who happened to be a student at the Technion.

I told him, with the entire class listening, "I dream of becoming a student at the Technion. What do you think I should do in order to make this dream come true?" It took bravery and vulnerability to express this dream aloud.

The teacher looked at me and said, "It's not for you. You'll never get admitted!"

You can only imagine how embarrassed and ashamed I was. I was devastated in front of the entire class, but I didn't give up on this dream. After a few years of hard work, I was admitted to the school and not only received my bachelor of science degree from the Technion, but my master's as well—with honors to boot. I wanted to send my diploma to this teacher but I never did. Perhaps I will send him a copy of this book. To see a lecture I gave at Technion with a very funny Mindsharing experiment, go to mindsharing.info/technion.

So how do we hold fast to our dreams when faced with discouragement or humiliation or a lack of validation? How do we keep from giving up? Many people do. The world is littered with people's discarded dreams. Perhaps if there had been Facebook when I was a teen, and I was able to share this dream with the crowd, I would have found the support I was lacking in school that day.

If you really want to know who a person is, ask them what they dream about, what they imagine but are afraid to say aloud, and what they would do if they knew they could not fail.

Ask this of yourself.

Then share it with your crowd.

If you have a dream and you have a big crowd of friends and

followers, you have a team in place to make your dreams come true. And if you have no idea what your dream is—ask your crowd to help you find it. Mindshare to discover your dreams, then Mindshare them into reality.

GO TO THE PRINCIPAL'S OFFICE

This picture was taken at my high school when I was fourteen years old. It was the only high school in my area that had a special class for computer programming. I knew that it was the only school for me.

You may be surprised to know this, but I was not the most popular kid in school. Things did not go well for me in this school. Being a geek back then was not cool at all. It was the opposite. I found myself with almost no friends. It took me years to understand that most of my teachers weren't good teachers. I was less than average in most areas except computer programming. I felt like quite a failure.

Recently I received a call from the principal of my old high school. I immediately felt like a kid who's being called to the principal's office. I wasn't sure what I had done wrong, but my heart pounded as if I were in big trouble. No matter what age you are, you never like getting a call from the principal.

To my relief, I hadn't done anything wrong; she just wanted me to come speak to a group of fourteen-year-old students. I accepted her invitation. I was excited to go back to my high school. It would be my way of erasing all those painful teenage memories.

The kids were amazing, and after my talk, I wrote this status on my Facebook page:

> I just finished presenting to a group of high school teenagers at my old high school. I told them that for me, high school was tough. I believed I wasn't smart, the teachers didn't like me, and the other kids thought I was strange.
>
> In the middle of my talk, a boy raised his hand and asked me why I had come back to the school if I had suffered so much here? I told him: "I didn't come here just to talk about crowd wisdom, although this is what I'm supposed to do. I'm here to tell you the things that no one told me when I was your age. If someone makes you feel that you're not good enough or talented enough, do me a favor and ignore that person. There's nothing you can't accomplish."

Basically, I told that boy what I wanted to hear when I was a kid. I told him what I wanted to hear when I first told Yosi about my dream. And I told him what the crowd had told me when they found out about my dream of standing on the TED stage.

After that talk, I received this e-mail from a girl in the audience. She allowed me to share her e-mail with my crowd.

Hi Lior,

Yesterday I attended your presentation. When you asked if we had a dream, I wanted to share my dream, but I was afraid of the reaction.

The dreams that my friends shared were "normal" like being a doctor or lawyer. These are professions in which almost anyone with a degree can find a job. They can make these dreams come true by investing time and effort in learning at school.

But my dream is harder to achieve and it's not just up to me.

Since I was very young, I always knew that I wanted to be involved with music. I've always loved to sing, play, and create. From the age of 12, I've taken voice lessons once a week and I've played the piano since I was eight. In the past year, I've come to understand that my dream will not come true, because I have a very small chance of succeeding in this profession.

My environment is not so supportive. No one sees me having a real future or a career in music.

I had given up on my dream and felt broken hearted. But after your lecture yesterday, I realized that if I do not go after my dream my future will be very frustrating, and maybe even wasted.

I have decided to not give up on my dream and not give
up until I make it come true.

I wanted to thank you for the amazing presentation.
Your story inspired me to not give up no matter what anyone around me says.

Thank you,

Yael [not her real name]

I know my crowd is there to inspire and support me in any
dream. And I believed that if I shared her e-mail with my crowd,
they might inspire and support her as well. I posted this to my
crowd along with her letter:

If someone wants to encourage her or give some good advice that might help fulfill her dream, you are invited to
respond. I'm sure she will read your comments in this
status. . . .

There is something magical that happens when you mix
Mindsharing with your dreams. My crowd responded as I
hoped they would. These are just a few of the many, many comments that Yael received in support of her dream.

- The thing about smart people is they seem like crazy
  people to dumb people.

- I'm a jazz player, piano teacher, and work with many art-
  ists. Here's my e-mail, you can contact me, and I'll try to
  help.

- Send her this quote from Michael Jordan: "I've missed
  more than nine thousand shots in my career. I've lost

almost three hundred games. Twenty-six times, I've been trusted to take the game winning shot and missed. I've failed over and over and over again in my life. And that is why I succeed."

- Yael, I managed the jazz and rock track at Talma Yalin high school. I've taught three thousand young musicians. Becoming a success in music is not harder than any other profession.

- My dear, your family just wants to protect you from disappointment and frustration. What they do not realize is that as long as you do not do what you want, you'll be disappointed and frustrated at every moment. What matters is what you believe. Do you believe them or do you believe in yourself? In the words of Henry Ford: "Whether you think you can or think you cannot, you're right."

There are times in our life when we need a crowd behind us. Cheering. Coaching. Telling us that it's okay to dream whatever crazy dream we have. When we Mindshare our dreams, the crowd becomes our biggest ally.

DREAMS EVOLVE

When I returned from my TED experience, many people asked me what my next dream would be. I answered in return, "What do you think that my next dream should be?" I hadn't thought about my next dream, until the crowd asked me this question.

I was still amazed that my first dream had happened so quickly with the help of the crowd.

And then I received this e-mail from a stranger.

Dear Lior,

I really enjoyed your talk at TED this year: it was moving, inspiring, and fascinating. I am a book and media agent, and I work with visionaries like Nelson Mandela, Richard Branson, neuroscientist Daniel Siegel, M.D., and many others on books that can create a wiser, healthier, and more just world. I think crowdsourcing is a very important part of the future, and I think you did a marvelous job of presenting it in a very accessible and exciting way.

I wonder if you might be interested in talking about creating a book based on many of the themes and topics covered in your talk. I've read *Wikinomics* and am familiar with Howe's *Crowdsourcing*, but would love to talk about whether there's room for something else, perhaps with a little more heart and soul, like your talk.

Let me know if this idea captures your imagination.

All the best,

Doug

I read it and thought to myself, a book? Someone wants to help me publish a book? I checked to see if the e-mail was addressed correctly.

And just that quickly—a new dream was born.

I call this dream *Mindsharing*.

I don't know how other authors approach writing a book, but I already had one crowd dream under my belt, so I knew exactly what to do. I turned to my crowd and asked them to join me in the process of writing this book.

Once I did that, all my fears (well, most of my fears) disappeared. I found myself surrounded by thousands of enthusiastic friends and followers eager to help make the dream of this book come true. The process for creating this book has been similar to the process of developing the TED talk. Similar, but a lot longer and with many more Mindsharing experiences.

The crowd has helped me find stories, edit my text, and overcome challenges. Writer's block, anyone? Yes, they have motivated and encouraged me. But they also have helped me to redefine my original dream and have shown me how that dream has evolved. My dream of speaking at TED was just a small part of a larger dream. My dream wasn't just to stand on a stage in Long Beach, it was to teach people, to inspire people, and to connect with people.

That dream of connection was born in me the very first time I logged in to that sysop and BBS as a child. It was there when I connected with people selling retail software as a teenager. It was there during my time at Microsoft when I found ways to connect people to products and reach out to them through marketing.

My dream is to be a teacher, and whether I teach from a stage, or a classroom, or a book is not what's important. My dream is to teach people just how powerful we are when we are connected to one another. When we think together. When we create together. The crowd has shown me that I am a serial dreamer. Someone who uses the power of Mindsharing to make his dreams come true, one dream after another, after another.

We evolve, and our dreams evolve, and then we evolve some more. I can't imagine a better way to live or to dream.

What's my next dream? My dream right now is that you will be inspired to dig out the dreams you had as a child and share them with the crowd. If this book inspires you to go after your dream, I'd love to hear about it at mindsharing.info/dream. Come and share your dream and read stories from other readers as they share their own dreams.

14.

DREAM A LITTLE DREAM WITH ME
(Crowd Coaching Dreams
into Reality)

Imagine you are a basketball player and it's the last seconds of the championship game. Your team is down by two and the coach calls a time-out and diagrams the play. A three-point shot that you will be the one to take. The coach then tells you that he believes in you, this is what you've worked so hard for all season, and it's your time and the team's time to shine. The time-out ends and you run onto the court. The crowd in the stands starts to cheer and yell and stomp their feet. They are telling you that they believe in you as well. The power of the crowd gives you energy and motivation. You take the shot. Three points. The buzzer sounds. The championship is won.

Now imagine this is in your everyday life. Imagine having a crowd of coaches diagramming your big plays in life and always believing in you. Imagine having your own personal, stadium-size crowd cheering you on and offering encouragement and motivation each time you're set up to take a big shot in life, regardless of whether you win or not. It might seem like a scary idea, at first. For some, their experience with large crowds is not a good one, and the idea of doing anything in front of a crowd brings up fear of failure, and feelings of shame, and presents a way of being vulnerable and exposed that is profoundly uncomfortable. We can love people and be terrified of them at the same time. People have the power to hurt us, and the crowd is made up of a lot of people. But remember the stats on Michael Jordan. He missed nine thousand shots, lost three hundred games, and failed to make the winning shot twenty-six times. He has failed over and over again, but he still had a crowd that supported him every step of the way.

When you are fearless enough to harness the force of the crowd to transform your dreams into reality, the result is nonstop crowd coaching, and what I like to call "crowd cheering."

As I sat down to write the final section of this book, I found myself staring at the computer screen. I couldn't write. I couldn't get all the stories and ideas out of my head, through my hands, and onto the page. I would just sit there. For hours. With nothing to show for it at the end of the day. I would try again the next day, and then the next day, and still blank.

This is when I started to panic. I would never meet my deadline. My book would never be published. My fears started to overwhelm me. I lost sleep. I was anxious.

This was more than writer's block—it was a creativity block. Days passed, deadlines were missed, and I knew I needed to make a change. A big change.

I went to the crowd and told them we have an obstacle in this dream we're creating. I'm stuck, I'm afraid, and I don't know what to do.

I received hundreds of ideas and suggestions. I also received more encouragement than I could believe. I may have been doubting myself, my creativity may have been absent, but the crowd believed in me and the crowd had all the creativity I needed.

Someone shared a link to a John Cleese video about creativity. It inspired me and made me laugh. Others invited me to come work in their homes and offices. Someone reminded me that creativity wasn't something you could lose, like car keys. And many, many people reminded me that they were waiting to read my book and they knew I wouldn't let them down.

It wasn't all words of encouragement, however; there was practicality in the crowd wisdom. The collective intelligence (what most people suggested) was for me to leave my office and go out and write somewhere else. They told me that instead of sitting in the same place where I write e-mails, and send invoices, and schedule meetings, I should go out and write from a place that was inspiring. A few said go to the woods. A few more said go to the mountains. But the majority said to go to the beach.

Here I was in the championship game and time was running out. My crowd diagrammed the play for me. Take your laptop. Go to a beach in Tel Aviv. Watch the sunset. Write.

This is your time to shine.

This is what you've worked hard for.

We're passing you the ball.

You take the shot.

Guess where I am right now as I write these words? I'm on the beach in a beautiful café. The sea is a deep blue color and the sky is clear. My iced coffee is delicious. Best of all—the words are flowing faster than they've ever flowed before.

My crowd coached me to success.

Your crowd can do the same for you.

A DIGITAL PUSH

In all the crucial and pivotal moments of turning my dreams into reality—identifying the dream, voicing the dream, taking action to accomplish my dream, overcoming obstacles, overcoming failures—the crowd was there as a collective coach. Telling me when to move right or move left. What plays to make and what fouls to avoid. The crowd was my coach and my cheering section. Often at the same time. Crowd coaching is an amazing phenomenon. A crowd can give you wisdom, as we've discussed throughout this book. It can help you improve your career and your personal life. But it is something else altogether when the crowd uses its power to propel you forward in the direction of your dreams. It creates a certain kind of intensity and momentum that is virtually impossible to achieve on your own.

It's a digital push forward.

This push is the value-added power and the dream-making catalyst that results from a life of Mindsharing.

The only other time in my life I've felt anything close to what it feels like to get a digital push was on my wedding day. At the ceremony, with my love, Ayala, by my side, we were surrounded by hundreds of our friends and family. Every person there had nothing but love for us, belief in us, and support for the great adventure we were embarking on. It felt as if we were flying high up in the sky.

It felt as if anything was possible.

This is what a digital push feels like. When you Mindshare your dreams with the crowd, and when the crowd coaches your dreams to success, it feels like it's your wedding day.

I can't think of any other time when so many people gather

together with nothing but love for a person. Wedding days and crowd coaching.

CROWD COACHING YOUR CAREER DREAMS

Ronen Koehler has had two long and successful careers. He was a submarine commander in the Israeli navy, and then he was a vice president at one of Israel's most successful high-tech companies, Check Point Software Technologies. Just as he turned fifty, Ronen decided it was time for him to think about the next chapter in his professional life. He was ready for a change. He just didn't know what it should be. Should he become a consultant? Or maybe go back to another management position? He didn't have a clue.

Over the years, his network on Facebook and LinkedIn had grown to be a few thousand strong. Some were friends, some were acquaintances, and some were friends of acquaintances. He had the perfect crowd for Mindsharing—big, diverse, and full of wisdom and power ready to be tapped.

He had never used this network for anything special or unusual. They were just there. Ronen had never really gotten all that social on his social networks.

Then one day he called me. He sounded a bit strange—not in a this-man-is-losing-his-mind way, but strange in a good way. He had just published a very special Facebook status. Ronen had just Mindshared his way into crowd dreaming and crowd coaching.

His status said that he had retired from Check Point, and that he was looking for the next big challenge in his life. Something he could do for the next ten or fifteen years. Then he did something that is quite hard for all of us to do: he admitted that he didn't know what to do and he asked for help. "Please share with me your ideas and your insights. What should my next career be?"

Ronen had taken one of the deepest and most personal decisions someone can have in their life, and turned it over to the crowd. He had asked the crowd to coach him on his next big move.

I asked him how he felt.

"I've never imagined how powerful this process could be for me," explained Ronen. "I am surrounded by so many people that know me from the past, and they are telling me how talented I am, and motivating me to dream big and do something challenging in the next phase of my life. I couldn't have ever imagined it would feel this way and be so positive. People really care about my choices, and are so positive about me finding my dream that it's making me work even harder to find out what my next dream might be."

Some people turn to a "life coach" or "career counselor" to help them figure out their next moves in life, or discover their passion and purpose. Ronen chose to use the crowd as his life coach. He received many ideas that he had never thought of before—people were even suggesting he go into politics. He also received a few job offers to lead inspiring organizations as CEO. There's something very powerful when more than one person tells you that you should do something. Suggestions move from opinion to wisdom.

This is Mindsharing at its finest.

Ronen, who had overseen close to three thousand employees at his last job, and was very familiar with the idea of mentoring or having a mentor, likened the experience to what he called "mega-mentoring." Not only were there many ideas and suggestions, people in his crowd were also inspired by his process of making a change and the courage he showed in asking the crowd for help. Crowd coaching has a domino effect. One time you are the player being coached, and the next time you are part of the coaching team.

CROWD SOOTHING

We all get afraid. Some of us are afraid of spiders. Some of us are afraid of heights. Some of us are afraid of change. A few years ago, my daughter Maya asked me if I could come do a presentation at her school. In her class. In front of all her friends. Of course, I immediately agreed—she's my daughter. And then I immediately panicked. Now, I've spoken on big stages and little stages, in front of thousands and in small groups. The one thing I had never done was a presentation in front of my daughter. And her friends.

I immediately turned into the awkward geek I thought I had left behind in high school. Or in college. Or at Microsoft. Okay, I was still an awkward geek and I didn't want my daughter to see me that way. At home, I was her hero. What if I disappointed her, or worse, embarrassed her in front of her friends? I couldn't do it. I wondered how I could call in sick to my own daughter.

I shared this fear with my Facebook friends. As soon as I did, the fear lost its power. As you can imagine, I received nothing but encouraging responses. The crowd gave me my confidence back. They coached it into me. They reminded me that not only could I do this presentation, and do it well, but it would be a special and unique experience that my daughter and I would remember forever.

Did I mention that Maya's friends now think she has the coolest dad ever?

Whenever I feel fear about something real or imagined, I can turn to my crowd and they will guide me through that fear. When hundreds of people tell you that you can do something, their voices drown out the voice of fear. The crowd replaces that fear with excitement and anticipation.

Sometimes we live our dreams and sometimes we live our fears. The biggest obstacle to making any dream come true is fear. Fear of the unknown. Fear of failure. This is what makes it so hard to step out of our comfort zone and into our dreams. When you rely on the crowd, facing your fears is easier. The crowd will empower you.

When you think of pursuing your dream, what are you afraid of?

What is your biggest fear?

You could pay a lot of money and go to a therapist to talk about your fears. You could hire a personal life coach and talk about your fears. Or you can go to your crowd and meet your fears head-on. No fear can stand up to the faith of the crowd.

Don't be afraid. Try it and you'll see.

CROWD MOTIVATION

I was in pain.

Now, I am something of a hypochondriac, but this was real pain. Abdominal pain that wouldn't go away. I went to see my doctor, who did a physical and took some blood tests. After the whooping cough debacle, she is now extra careful to ensure that I get exhaustive testing. She knows I have Dr. Crowd on speed dial.

The results were not good. "Lior," she said, "it's time to change the way you live your life. You are living in the body of a fifty-year-old. You don't exercise. You eat too much junk food. Enough is enough. You need to get a grip on yourself if you wish to live a healthy and long life."

I was surprised. I was only forty-two, and I enjoyed living my life without having to put time and effort into exercising. I loved my junk food. Who has time to eat healthy anyway?

But the doctor's words had frightened me. I had a lot still to achieve in life, and I had young children. I needed to get healthy. I left her office vowing to change my ways.

I started a diet for the first time in my life, and I began walking every day for thirty minutes. In a few months, my energy and stamina increased. I was seeing results. I felt good. It took a year, but I lost twenty-nine pounds and ran a 10K at the Tel Aviv Marathon.

People tell me I look like a young Brad Pitt.

Not really. But they do tell me I look ten years younger.

I posted pictures from the Tel Aviv Marathon, and I was overwhelmed by the amount of positive comments I received. It felt great to get all the cheers and congratulations and virtual hugs.

It made me realize that I had made a big mistake. I could have used all that support at the beginning, during those difficult days when I was just starting to exercise and I didn't think it would ever get easier. If I had shared my journey with the crowd from the beginning rather than just from the finish line, they could have helped me so much. They could have cheered for me all along and made the journey that much easier to bear.

It's the motivation we get from those around us that enables us to overcome challenges. Whether we are trying to lose weight, eat healthier, exercise more, or overcome an addiction, support is the most critical determinant of our success and has

even been shown to lessen our physical pain. Patients with heart or lung disease participating in a support group reported a mean pain reduction of 20 percent compared with those who didn't participate in group support.[1] Breast cancer patients who participated in group psychotherapy had twice the survival rate of patients who didn't meet in groups.[2] Social support is critically important. When people get emotional support from people they trust, they change their behavior.[3] Research shows that social support is associated with better immune function, lower stress, and lower blood pressure.

There are many support groups available online. When comparing the effect of online support groups with physical meetings, researchers found that online and face-to-face support groups have a similar positive effect on patients.[4] Twelve-step groups have been utilizing the benefits of group support for decades, and this support reaches around the globe.

The bottom line is we are stronger together, whether we connect face-to-face or through social media. As we discussed in the beginning, we are wired for connection. It's how we evolved. We heal together, and Mindsharing offers a new tool for healing in this way.

This is what crowd coaching is all about.

So why didn't I initially share my journey with the crowd?

Me. Mr. Mindshare. The person who takes his temperature on a video blog and shares it with the crowd.

The truth is, I didn't have the courage to share what my doctor told me. I was afraid, and I didn't go to the crowd to help me walk through my fear or walk with me on my journey to healthier living. I was embarrassed. I felt too vulnerable.

We all struggle with challenges. We all have things we need or want to change about ourselves. We all have days when we lack motivation, or willpower. There are just some days when eating a dozen doughnuts seems like a really good idea. There are times when we feel we are at our weakest and most vulnerable.

These are the times we need our crowd the most.

PERSONAL REBOOT

Jeff Pulver is a friend of mine. Well, Jeff has a lot of friends. More than 120,000 friends and followers on Facebook, and 500,000 followers on Twitter. He's a very friendly guy. Whenever I see him, I just want to give him a big hug.

Jeff also struggled with his weight. In early 2012, Jeff weighed 334 pounds. He couldn't sleep more than an hour or two straight. He was also struggling with a number of personal issues that added to the heaviness he carried.

One day he went to go scuba diving and couldn't fit into a wet suit. He was constantly in physical pain, but he kept it to himself. As an investor, he would meet with many professionals and entrepreneurs. One day he sent an e-mail to a woman and asked for a meeting. It wasn't a date, just a regular business meeting. She mistakenly thought it was for a personal meeting and e-mailed him back, apologetically saying she couldn't meet with him because he was too fat.

Ouch. Even more pain for Jeff.

Jeff knew he had to make a big change and went to see a doctor. He asked the doctor about getting gastric bypass surgery, secretly hoping the doctor would say there was no need for something that radical and things were not that bad. The doctor said it was a good idea.

That's when Jeff really knew his situation was not good. Not good at all.

He met with a friend who advised him to "bypass the bypass" and try working out instead. Jeff began to exercise, but at 334 pounds, he couldn't do much. He started working out for five minutes a day, every few days. That's it. After his brief workout, he would go have a nice breakfast.

Jeff bought forty-one books on the subject of health and fitness. Forty-one! He read many of them, and decided to join a gym. He lost 15 pounds. It wasn't much, and it wasn't a big percentage of his 334 pounds, but it was a nice start. He didn't tell anyone about what he was trying to do. He kept it a secret.

Eventually he confided in a friend who told him, "Share what you're doing with your Facebook and Twitter followers. That way, you won't be able to disappoint them."

His friend was right. No one wants to disappoint 500,000 people.

Still, Jeff was afraid. It felt way too personal, like he would be standing naked in front of a crowd of people. But 500,000 people equals a lot of people who could both encourage him and hold him accountable. Jeff summoned up his courage and bravely went where I was afraid to go.

On October 22, 2012, Jeff shared honestly with his Facebook friends about the difficult situation he was in. He called his post "Nothing Is Impossible—My Personal Reboot." It took him more than an hour to write it, and a whole lot of bravery to share it.

Then he shared his dream. His dream was to lose at least one hundred pounds, gain muscle, and do a one-armed push-up at a big conference he was hosting in a year.

It was a bold move and a big dream. But Jeff had thrown the gauntlet down to his friends. And his friends accepted the challenge. He was overwhelmed by hundreds of comments and private messages. It was in that moment that Jeff realized social media is for way more than sharing. It was a source of motivation and inspiration. Jeff had just invited the crowd into his dream, and was about to get the digital push of a lifetime.

"The support I received was absolutely amazing. I've never

experienced so much love and support. It was deeply impactful. One day I was at the SXSW conference and Walt Mossberg from *The Wall Street Journal* saw me and said, 'You're doing great, Jeff.' Ever since then, I find myself now tweeting and posting more about my personal life than I do about technology."

Jeff was experiencing firsthand the incredible power and magic that happens when we Mindshare.

I asked Jeff how he would describe the feeling of getting motivated by the crowd to someone who had never felt it. He gave me a beautiful answer.

"Imagine that you're running in an empty street as part of a race and you're all by yourself. When you're Mindsharing and getting motivated by your own crowd, it's as if you're running and the streets are full of people with signs and posters to cheer you on. You see people you know and people you don't know. The crowd is at least five people deep on either side, and they are all there to support you. When you Mindshare, you are never alone."

Jeff lost more than 110 pounds in a year. And he did his one-armed push-up at the conference. The crowd not only motivated him to achieve his dream, they helped him surpass his dream.

I recently asked this amazing high-tech wizard what his greatest insight was about his crowd-dreaming journey. I think of his words often.

"Being afraid is very normal, but being vulnerable might be your biggest strength. That's true in entrepreneurship as well as in our personal lives. It's easier said than done, but this is the truth. Be open and use social media to share things that scare you the most. This is true courage. This is what will give you so much strength and change your life forever." (You can see a

video of Jeff Pulver's TEDx talk, where he tells his story in more detail, at mindsharing.info/pulver.)

Vulnerability may be our greatest strength in the age of Mindsharing. When we acknowledge our true interdependence, and the profound connection we have with one another, and embrace the technology that allows this connection to flourish—we can do absolutely anything.

We can Mindshare our careers.

We can Mindshare our personal lives.

We can Mindshare our dreams.

We can Mindshare our future.

Together we can walk through any fear, face any challenge, and live lives that are more joyous and more fulfilling than we ever imagined.

But don't just take my word for it.

Ask the crowd what they think.

When you are done, take the advice I was given before I stepped onto the TED stage. It's the last bit of advice given to every TED speaker with an idea worth spreading.

"Shine a light—illuminate the beautiful and simplify the complex. Tell a story. Bravely bare your soul, your passion, your hopes, and your fears. Prepare for impact, a wondrous attentive throng awaits you."

As you practice the art of crowdsourcing everything, and unlock the potential for Mindsharing in your own life, remember these last words of advice, and prepare for the impact Mindsharing will have in your life.

The crowd is waiting for you.

CONCLUSION: The Future of Mindsharing

I t is 1984.

I walked out of the movie theater in awe, and feeling as if I were in another world. I suspiciously eyed the people around me. What if everyone around me was a robot? Who were the good robots and who were the bad robots? What if there was a Terminator sent from the future? Who would save the day when the time came for man to go up against machine?

I knew the answer to that question, and it filled me with pride. Even at the age of fourteen, before there were laptops, or the Internet, or smart phones, I knew the truth. In the future, the geeks would save the world.

I just hoped there would be cool robots walking around when it happened.

I loved that first *Terminator* movie. I couldn't wait to see what the future had in store. I remember watching through Arnold Schwarzenegger's robot eyes, seeing him analyze complicated images in real time. What amazing technology that would be. It was thrilling to imagine.

In 1984, I would often wonder if thirty years into the future we would have flying cars, time travel machines, and superhuman abilities. Guess what? We do.

In 2012, the Aeromobil flying car was designed and the prototype took flight for the first time. As far as time travel is concerned, physicists have found that time is slower on earth than it is on the Global Positioning System satellites in space. And let's not even get started on quantum mechanics, rotating black holes, or wormholes. But what about superhuman abilities? How many years in the future before we all evolve with superpowers?

Or does Mindsharing give us our superpowers now?

Facial image recognition is complicated, but the technology has improved dramatically in recent years. With Mindsharing, we don't need a robotic eye to analyze a complicated image. Four Harvard School of Engineering and Applied Sciences researchers have published research and developed an app that does the same thing as Arnold Schwarzenegger's eyeball in *The Terminator*. The app is called PlateMate, and it allows you to take a picture of your meal and get an instant analysis of the meal's calories, fat, protein, and other nutritional components. How does it do this? Through Mindsharing. The picture of the meal is sent to Amazon Mechanical Turk, where the crowd provides the breakdown in real time. Much like estimating the weight of an ox, untrained Turkers are able to give a nutritional breakdown nearly as accurate as that of expert dietitians.[1]

What about a future where we wear smart glasses that take video of wherever we are and whatever we are doing? In one click, we get the nutritional content of our food, another click and we get dating advice from the crowd in real time, in the next click we get an alert that we are in danger. When we are connected to the crowd, our superpowers grow exponentially.

WHAT'S YOUR NQ?

I told you the story about how my child tried to touch a picture on the front of the newspaper and became upset when it wouldn't come to life. Recently, my youngest child walked up to the television in our house and also tried to turn it on by touching the screen. He couldn't understand why it didn't work like the iPad he was used to.

Our children are being born in the digital age, an age that is evolving faster than we are. Elementary school children are navigating the world of social media with ease—managing their own Instagram accounts, uploading videos to YouTube, and using FaceTime and Skype to speak to relatives around the globe. What's complicated to those of us who grew up with the Dewey Decimal System is second nature to the new generations of digital natives. As they grow, they will demand technology to grow with them, and if it doesn't, they will invent what they need.

Human beings are becoming more intelligent over time. It's called the Flynn effect. According to research, every decade, the average IQ scores increase. In the future, I see a world where intelligence is measured a little differently. What if we factor our own intelligence with the intelligence of our crowd or network?

Currently there are several online services trying to measure the power we gain based on the size of our crowd. One of these services is Klout (www.klout.com). Klout is an analytics tool that ranks people according to their online social influence and gives a corresponding "Klout Score." What if our NQ, or network quotient (a term coined by Tom Boyle of British Telecom^2), was more important than our IQ? When we add our NQ to our IQ, how much does our intelligence increase? Mindsharing is how we raise our NQ score.

We are more intelligent together, and in the future, perhaps our intelligence will be measured more by our connections to one another than by our intelligence as individuals. With Mindsharing, our NQ is more critical to our success than our IQ. It is the great equalizer of the future.

CONNECTING THE GLOBAL BRAIN

The cerebral cortex is the area in the brain that relates directly to human intelligence. It has ten billion connected neurons working together to create our intelligence. With seven billion people in the world, imagine what we could create if each of those seven billion brains were connected.

The math is as staggering as the possibilities.

Could we create a global brain? Right now, with more than one billion users, Facebook connects the largest number of people (and brains) together in a way that enables them to engage with one another and think together. But Facebook is selective, you have to be friends to think collectively, and the social network limits the number of friends to five thousand. What if this were opened up? What if we freed a billion brains on Facebook to come together and Mindshare?

Is this the future?

LEADERS WHO MINDSHARE

When it comes to technology, Steve Jobs was a true leader—a genius who created technological breakthroughs that have changed our lives forever. He was one of the people who have led us into a future only imagined in science fiction movies.

A true leader.

As we travel farther into a future of Mindsharing, perhaps we will see our governments and our leaders relying more on the power of the crowd to make their decisions. Mindsharing is democracy 2.0. Let's judge our future politicians and leaders not on their own genius, but on how well they tap into the genius of the people—the crowd.

Will we someday value a leader for his humility? For his vulnerability? For his ability to know that he's not smarter than the people he leads? In the future my vote will be cast not for the man or woman who inspires me to vote for him or her, but for the leader who inspires me to think with him or her. Let's not determine an election by the popular vote, let's determine elections by the Mindsharing vote. I trust the leader who says, "I don't know the answer to that, let me ask the people." This is democracy at its finest. Don't show me the politician who can shake the most hands, or kiss the most babies, or make the most promises. Show me the politician who can gather the most collective intelligence. I will vote for the person who can Mindshare.

WE ARE STRONGER THAN ME

There is no way to know what the future holds. I do believe that Mindsharing is the key to our future. Thinking together, we can solve some of our world's greatest problems, and in our future, ensure the future of our children, and their children, and many generations to come.

I imagine someday my grandchildren saying, "Did you know that when Grandpa Lior was a kid, people used to think by themselves?" It's the same as when I tell my children that when I was in school we had to go to the library to look up information. It didn't just appear in front of us. That would have seemed like magic or a science fiction movie.

I hope that when my grandchildren search the Internet, the results come from a search engine that gives only the collective wisdom of the crowd. A Mindsharing database that provides the best answer to any question as determined by the intelligence of the global brain.

Google, are you listening? Get on it.

When that time comes, I imagine my grandchildren (or great-grandchildren) laughing about the time when people actually had to read a book to learn how to Mindshare.

Actually, I don't have to imagine. I will just take my flying car on over to my time travel machine and tell them about it myself.

But don't worry.

I'll be back.

And then together, we will Mindshare our way into a future more brilliant than anything we could ever imagine on our own.

I invite you to join my crowd, and contribute to the Mindsharing conversation. Let me know how Mindsharing is working in your life, and the future you envision. *We* are always stronger than *me*.

I invite you to send me an e-mail at liorz@live.com or join mindsharing.info. Share your story, your thoughts about Mindsharing, and your experience reading this book.

My crowd and I are waiting to hear from you.

And remember, great minds think alike, clever minds think together.

ACKNOWLEDGMENTS

This book was created using Mindsharing with thousands of people. But before acknowledging them, I wanted to start by thanking two amazing people who created this book with me and were a huge part of this incredible journey I've been on.

My first and foremost thank-you is to Lara Love Hardin, my partner in writing this book. We've spent countless hours together in which I've learned to admire and adore her gift with words. If writing a book is like having a baby—although the pregnancy is longer than nine months—then Lara is the proud mother. Lara, thank you for your amazing work and friendship. You have a very special place in my heart.

Mindsharing is a special baby, as it has two fathers. My second huge thank-you is to my literary agent and *Mindsharing*'s second father, Doug Abrams. His exceptional vision, insight, and guidance made this book possible. Doug, I am so fortunate to have you as my friend and mentor. Thank you for transforming *Mindsharing* from a dream into a reality.

A big thank-you to the wonderful team of professionals at Portfolio: my editor, Maria Gagliano, and publisher, Adrian Zackheim, along with Rachel Moore, Will Weisser, Stefanie Rosenblum, Tara McBride, Victoria Miller, Jesse Maeshiro, and many others who make up this hardworking team.

I'd like to thank David Passig, my PhD professor, for intro-ducing me to the fascinating world of crowd wisdom, and for being my mentor and inspiration.

To Peter Diamandis and Jeff Pulver for supporting *Mind-sharing* from the very beginning. And to my friends who inspired me to write a book, Ilan Itzhayek, Dov Alfon, Gideon Amichay, Gil Peretz, Michael Weiz, and Abigail Tennenbaum.

I also want to thank Maya Elhalal-Levavi for changing my life by letting me know about TED auditions; Aya Shapir for giving me the name *Mindsharing*; and Or Sagy for suggesting I bring an ox on the TED stage. To Chris Anderson, Kelly Stoetzel, June Cohen, and the entire team at TED for inviting me to speak on the TED stage.

Among the thousands of people who were a part of creating this book, a few stand out because they invested many hours in editing the book while adding their thoughtful insights. Thank you Arod Ballisa, Saviram Lior, Noam Ilovich, Daphna Joffe, and Sorin Solomon.

To Jonathan Klinger for his wonderful legal advice and per-sonal story that gave me great insights about Mindsharing for love.

To Sharon Alon and the wonderful team at Herods Tel-Aviv for their generous invitation to write at their hotel while being inspired by the Tel Aviv seashore.

A very special thank-you to my former managers and mentors, Arie Scope, Shimon Zacks, Meir Raz, Aliza Tamir, Danny Yamin, Adi Eyal, and Judi Granit for helping me to grow out of my comfort zone.

To my private crowd of close friends who are always there for me, Erez and Nava Simon, Rami and Iris Joseph, Yosi and Gili Taguri, Eran and Einat Arbel.

I'd like to thank my family, whom I love with all my heart. My parents, Varda and Moshe. My brothers, Liat and Gal. My wonderful in-law, Abraham. My children, Maya, Ori, and Assaf, and my wife and best friend, Ayala. You are the love of my life and the reason I'm in this world.

People typically think that writers create out of their own imagination. The reality is that *Mindsharing* is the product of thousands of brilliant people who came together to create a crowdsourced book about crowdsourcing. At the end of the book there's a list of all those who contributed (and that I managed to keep track of). For everyone who was part of creating *Mindsharing*—thank you so much. I could not have done this without you.

I am only as good as my crowd.

I wish to dedicate this book to the memory of my amazing mother-in-law, Sara Toledano. I wish that I had known the power of Mindsharing while she was ill—perhaps I could have used this power to save her life.

ACKNOWLEDGMENTS TO MY CROWD

These are members of my crowd who took an active role in reading, editing, giving suggestions, and helping. The wisdom in this book first and foremost belongs to their collective intelligence, passion, and enthusiasm to create a crowdsourced book about crowdsourcing.

Thank you all!

A

Ilanit Aba
Noya Abramovich
Eyal Adanya
Xen Mendelsohn Aderka
Hadas Adler
Ron Ahronson
Eliav Alaluf
Tomer Ablkosh
Asaf Alexanderovitch
Dina Alfasi
Itsik Alfon
Asaf Almog
Beatrice Almog
Eran Alshech
Yanir Alter

Anat Amely
Lior Cohen Amikam
Alon Amir
Ariel Amit
Ruthy Amrani
Moti Anav
Meir Ansher
Hila Granot Antebi
Idan Arbiv
Michael Arens
Ari+Ella
Yael Ariel
Edelman Arik
Noam Armonn
Dana Ashkenazi
Ofek Ashkenazy

Yoni Assia
Amos Atia
Nadav Avidan
Doron Avidar
Galit Avinoam
Dor Aviran
Yaniv Avital
Lior Avitan
Elad Aviv
Liran Aviv
Adi Avnit
Amir Avnon
Galit Azar
Limor Azulay

B

Itamar B
Arod Balissa
Danny Baltuch
Amit Banayan
Dany Bar
Tal Bar
Galit Barash
Ohad Barash
Maya Barda
Michal Bareket
Miki Barkan
Shira Levy Barkan
Sarid Bar Meir
Alon Barnea
Sahar Bar-Nissan
Matan Bar Sela
Ilanit Bar-Zeev
Yariv Bash
Ishay Bason
Roni Bass
Karina Batat

Gabby Begas
Yossi Behar
Sharon Beilis
Roy Ben-Alta
Yaniv Ben Atia
Motti Ben David
Arik Ben-Dov
Yfat Ben Elissar
Ari Ben-Ephraim
Roei Ben Gal
Ron Ben-Haim
Dori Ben Israel
Doron Benita
Hanna Ben Menachem
Erez Ben-Moshe
Itzik Ben-Shitrit
Michal Shargil Ben Sira
Shay Ben Yaakov
Eyal Ben-Ze'ev
Moti Berkovitz
Alina Bernstein
Ady Bertschneider
Inbal Betzer
Rinat Bialer
Hadas Ariel Blankchtein
Israel Blechman
Dana Bloch
Rotem Bonder
Opher Brayer
Elhanan Brisk
Ofaz Brisker
Billie Broaris
Margalit Brock
Yanush Budnitzky
Andrey Bukati

C

Joel Califa
Leah Calo
Nir Cats
Dr. Gil Chapnick
Gilad Chatsav
Gilad Chazav
Maor Chen
Moshik Chen
Narkiss Chen
Yaron Chervin
Amira Cohen
Arale Cohen
Clara Cohen
Eran Cohen
Izak Cohen
Meytal Cohen
Michal Cohen
Noa Cohen
Rami Cohen
Ran Cohen
Tomer Cohen
Yoram Cohen
Gal Corfas

D

Allon Dafner
Dor Dali
Yossi Dan
Adi Daniel
Saray Danmias
Shelly Danosh
Aviram Dar
Monika Bercu David
Frida Dayan
Yuli Desiatnikov
Ron Deutsch

Yeshayau Deutsch
Zachi Diner
Ehud Dinerman
Shimon Doodkin
Lior Dori
Nir Dori
Eyal Doron
Carmit Dotan
Ronit Doyev
Eran Dror
Yoni Dror
Nadav Drori
Itai Druckmann
Shirry Harpaz-Dvir

E

Ziv Eden
Dikla Edlis
Guy Einy
Ori Eisen
Ami Elazari
Liron Elbaz
David Elharar
Einat Eliash
Sandra Eliash
Amir Elion
Yair Engel
Libit Even-Paz
Adi Eyal
Ofer Eyni

F

Michal Falk
Roi Fainstein
Anat Fanti
Esther Feffer
Benjamin Feinstein

Bella Feld
Elad Feldman
Ofer Feldman
Eran Ferri
Micahel Fingerhut
Iris Fink
Shiri Fisher
Dooby Flink
Gilad Flint
Sendi Frangi
Igot Frenkel
Yonatan Frenkel
Carlos Freund
Avi Friedland-Zion
Dan Friedman
Dana Friedman
David Friedman
Sagi Frishman
Dan Frommer

G
Ella Gabai
Ronen Gafni
Dani Galil
Udi Galili
Rotem Ganor
Yonatan Gat
Ilan Gattegno
Eran Gefen
Udi Gelbort
Inbal Gelfarb
Orly Geva
Hadas Raz Gilboa
Itzik Gini
Noa Gottfrief
Eti Golan
Giora Golan

Noam Gold
Igor Goldfeld
Ofir Goldman
Yaacov Goldman
Uri Gordon
Dvir Goren
Tammy Goren
Uri Goren
Ariel Gottlieb
Barak Gozner
Judi Granit
Iffat bar-kol Grecht
Erez Greenberg
Inbal Shani Greenberg
Merav Greenzweig
Jacob Grinshpan
Yaacov Grinshpan
Dan Gross
Einat Gross
Gady Grosz
Anat Gur
Alon Gur-Arie
Tamar Guy

H
Eliea Alon Hacohen
Shimon Hacoon
Danny Hadad
Lior Hadari
Ronen Hadas
Adina Hagege
Aviad Hahami
Sarit Haim
Neriad Hakak
Ron Haklai
Shahar Halperin
Almog Tal Ben Hamo

Amir Hanan
Amir Haramaty
Michal Bleiman Harari
Yorav Harel
Roni Kenet Harmelin
Shachar Hefetz
Vardit Hemo
Limor Henig
Yifah Hermony
Sachar Hevrony
Neomi Heyman
Shiri Hirsch
Anat Hlfin
Nir Hoff
Jermy Hoffman
Nissim Hofi
Tamir Huberman

I

Yafit Ido-Greenapple
Elinor Igal
Idan Igali
Noam Ilovich
Ronen Inbar
Ilan Itzhayek

J

Efi Jeremiah
Daphna Joffe

K

Amir Kaldor
Erez Kalev
Yael Kalinsky
Ravit Kalod
Ahuva Kamar
Ronit Kamay

Yosi Kan
Yoel Kaplan
Keren Kapulsky
Moshe Karasik
Maya Karmely
Gina Kass
Meir Kaufman
Noy Kedem
Israel Kehat
Meirav Keinan
Omri Keli
Amir Keren
Granit Keren
Evgeny Klainer
Rami Kleiman
Carmit Klein
Inbar Klein
Anat Klumel
Gali Knobel
Hilel Kobrovski
Reuven Kogan
Eran Kolber
Hila Koren
Lior Koren
Liran Kotzer
Orly Krieger
Moti Krispil
Nurit Kruk-Zilca
Yoav Kula

L

Amit Lahav
Limor Lahiani
Keren Landau
Sarital Landesman
Shai Cohen Laor
Vered Lasri

Itzik Lavi
Vicky Meshel Lavi
Shmulik Lederman
Bat-Zion Leibovitch
Orly Leon
Hanan Lev
Yuval Lev
Maya Elhalal Levavi
Orit Arkin Levi
Yossi Levi
Michal Levin
Mor Levin
Natanel Levis
Pazit Levitan
Anat Calo Levron
Ezy Levy
Ilan Levy
Meny Levy
Mikey Levy
Natan Levy
Shani Levy
Nir Lewy
Omer Lewy
Doron Libshtein
Dan Lichtenfeld
Itay Lichtenzon
Dafna Lifshitz
Saviram Lior
Israel Litman
Revital Cohen Liverant
Dean Livne
Dror Liwer
Alisa Lutski
Amir Luz
Slava Luzakin

M

Yuval Machlin
Ran Magen
Ruth Maller
Dorin Mandelbaum
Erez Manhaimer
Tzahi Manistersky
Asaf Manor
Yoram Marciano
Gady Margalit
Mali Marton
Allon Mason
Sharon Mass
Daniel Matalon
Alon Matas
Aviv Matsa
Beto Maya
Dan Mayzlish
Orly Melamed
Tina Meerry Melusyan
Reut Menashe
Shachar Mendelboim
Itzhaki Merav
Rami Michaeli
Maya Miller
Talia Miller
Liron Milo
Yanai Milstein
Daria Mirkurbanova
Michael Mishan
Niso Missistrano
Hila Mitzner
Dan Mor
Yigal Mor
Daniel Moran
Adrian Moskovitch
Guy Moskowitz

Hagit Movshovitz
Avigaile Moyal

N
Dana Nachmias
Eliran Nagar
Sarit Naziri
Tami Neuthal
Teddy Neuwirth
Galia Nevo
Tal Ninio
Rotem Nissim
Avishay Niv
Iris Noti
Tomer Novotny

O
Tamar Obrasky
Daniel Ohaion
Etti Okon
Sharon Call Or
Smadar Or
Zen Ore
Aviya Oren
Gila Oren
Lev Oren
Gal Oz

P
Orni Pachman
Avishay Pariz
Gal Pasternak
Daniel Samuel Patrick
Dor Pazuelo
Yuval Pecht
Yael Pedhatzur
Yael Peleg

Shlomi Perez
Kobi Pinker
Ran Pinker
Tzipi Pinkus
Amir Pinto
Meir Pinto
Dror Pipano
Hagai Pipko
Shirley Pollak
Ilya Polonsky
Limor Poran
Michael Poroger
Roy Povarchik
Itai Preis
Yuval Pridan

R
Amit Raam
Rami Rachamim
Einat Raiff
Yaniv Raphael
Raz Rarush
Ella Rashkovich
Ariel Rattner
Daniel Ravner
Barak Raz
Lital Raz
Alon Refael
Benny Reich
Shachar Reichman
Yogev Reinhold
Idit Reiss
Ofer Reiss
Yair Restatcher
Tal Reuven
Gal Righter
Ofir Rob

Ronit Benbasat Rom
Adi Romem
Noam Ron
Ofir Ron
Guy Ronen
Mel Rosenberg
Barak Roth
Ohad Roth
Inbal Asif Rothman
Danny Roup
Menachem Rozenblum
Dany Rubinshtein
Haim Rubinstein
Assis Ruth

S
Helit Saad
Shimon Saban
Hanoch Sachar
Moti Sachrai
Merav Sadovsky
Maya Sagi
Uriel Samson
Gerry Sapir
Tal Sarid
Gilad Sasson
Uri Savran
Hamutal Schieber
Asaph Schulman
Doron Schwartz
Ron Schwartz
Yitzhack Schwartz
Arie Scope
Ori Segol
Tom Sela
Ronen Shaal
Lidia Shaddow

Roi Shahaf
Batia Shaham
Hans Shakur
Ariana Shalem
Hilel Shalev
Orna Shalomof
Dani Shames
Anat Shani
Sagi Shani
Sarit Shani
Aya Shapir
Daffy Shapir
Daniel Shapiro
Irit Sharabani
Amit Sharky
Sigal Shavit
Shalev Shelly
Tamar Shen-Orr
Ronny Sherer
Rakefet Shfaim
Nir Shilo
Roie Shiloah
David Shimon
Itay Shiner
Asaf Shmaya
Nedira Shmueli
Shlomit Shohat
Li Aviram Shoshani
Zack Silbinger
Guy Simhon
Guy Simon
Mazi Solomon
Sorin Solomon
Galit Solomonov
Vladimir Soroka
Hilla Srour
Ron Stern

Ran Styr
Tal Surasky

T

Uri Tagger
Yosi Taguri
Ayelet Tal
Shevik Tal
Aliza Tamir
Sarit Tamir
Orit Tati
Ilana Tavor
Diana Tenne
Iris Ticher
Liora Titinger
Smadar Torres
Or Tsviely
David Tuchfeld
Shai Tzefadia
Yonit Tzuk

V

Marina Vaknin
Oded Valin
Racheli Vanunu
Ronit Vardi
Shani Verbel
Raya Volinsky
Sharon Gonen-Volkovich

W

Yael Wagner
Ayelet Webber-Zvik
Razia Weisselberg
Vered Wolff

Y

Yaniv Yaakubovich
Avi Yafe
Malkah Yair
Danny Yamin
Guy Yanai
Ola Yasinovi
Ido Yavnai
Ronen Yechi Yechieli
Hagai Yedidya
Or Yeger
Uri Yehidi
Assaf Younger
Yifat Yudevsky
Matan Yungman
Eitan Yurman

Z

Shimon Zacks
Tal Zaibert
Mordehai Zaitler
Adi Zamir
Rachel Zamir
Erez Zehavi
Mordechai Zeitler
Pavel Zeldin
Shlomi Zigart
Gai Zomer
Ziggi Zukerman
David Zusiman
Noga Zweigenberg

MINDSHARING RESOURCES

There are hundreds of Web sites that enable you to actively practice Mindsharing or get aggregated wisdom from big crowds. Here is a list of Web sites that appear in the book and other Web sites I find to be useful when Mindsharing. Many of them also have an app for your smart phone so that you can Mindshare on the go. For a complete and updated list of Mindsharing resources, please visit mindsharing.info/resources.

HOW TO REACH ME

liorz@live.com
   My personal e-mail address

mindsharing.info
   Mindsharing official Web site

facebook.com/mind.sharing.book
   Mindsharing official Facebook page

facebook.com/lior.zoref
   My personal Facebook page

twitter.com/liorz
   On Twitter, why don't you follow me?

instagram.com/liorz
My photo stream on Instagram

GENERAL Q&A

quora.com
The most sophisticated platform for Q&A

answers.yahoo.com
Probably the first Q&A platform

ted.com/conversations
Q&A around big ideas and big dreams

patientslikeme.com
A real-time research platform and large network

crowdmed.com
Solve the world's most difficult medical cases

fold.it
Help find a cure while playing a game called Foldit

treato.com
Patient intelligence based on real-life experiences

FUNDING

kickstarter.com
Fund a creative project

indiegogo.com
Fund any project

DESIGN

99designs.com
Get a design—from a logo to a book cover

designcrowd.com
The same as above

istockphoto.com
   Stock photos, illustrations, video, and audio

KNOWLEDGE

wikipedia.org
   Well . . . we all know Wikipedia

reddit.com
   News and interesting stories

FINANCE

billguard.com
   Smart phone app to protect your credit cards

etoro.com
   A social investment network

SOLVE BUSINESS PROBLEMS

innocentive.com
   Solve problems by offering rewards

ideabounty.com
   Get or give a creative idea for business

utest.com
   Software testing

mturk.com
   Give a small task to a big crowd

SOCIAL NETWORKS READY FOR MINDSHARING

facebook.com
   Mindshare with your friends

twitter.com
   Mindsharing for short questions

linkedin.com
  Crowd wisdom from professionals

klout.com
  Rank influence of social media users

OTHER

community.babycenter.com
  Get parenting advice from the crowd

fiverr.com
  A crowdsourced marketplace for services

glassdoor.com
  Find jobs and gain insights about companies

xprize.com
  Encourage technological development

globalcrowd.com
  U.S. government intelligence forecasting

cci.mit.edu
  MIT Center for Collective Intelligence

crowdsourcing.org
  Crowdsourcing industry news

NOTES

INTRODUCTION: THE POWER OF WE

1. Eduardo Andrade and Dan Ariely, "The Enduring Impact of Transient Emotions on Decision Making," *Organizational Behavior and Human Decision Processes* 109 (2009): 1–8.
2. I. D. Couzin, "Collective Cognition in Animal Groups," *Trends in Cognitive Sciences* 13(1) (2009): 36–43.
3. M. Granovetter, "The Strength of Weak Ties," *American Journal of Sociology* 78(6) (1973): 1.
4. Nicholas A. Christakis and James H. Fowler, *Connected: The Surprising Power of Our Social Networks and How They Shape Our Lives* (Hachette Digital, Inc., 2009).
5. J. D. Montgomery, "Job Search and Network Composition: Implications of the Strength-of-Weak-Ties Hypothesis," *American Sociological Review* 57 (October 1992): 586–96.
6. Francis Galton, "Vox Populi," *Nature* 75 (1907): 450–51.

CHAPTER 1: FINDING YOUR CROWD

1. C. Wagner and T. Vinaimont, "Evaluating the Wisdom of Crowds," *Issues in Information Systems* 11(1) (2010): 724–32.

CHAPTER 2: THE NEW NETWORK

1. http://www.reddit.com/r/resumes.
2. http://www.glassdoor.com/Best-Places-to-Work-LST_KQ0,19 .htm (August 2014).
3. http://www.glassdoor.com/Interview/index.htm.

4. http://www.npr.org/blogs/parallels/2014/04/02/297839429/-so
    -you-think-youre-smarter-than-a-cia-agent.
5. http://goodjudgmentproject.com/blog/?p=87.
6. http://www.npr.org/blogs/parallels/2014/04/02/297839429/-so
    -you-think-youre-smarter-than-a-cia-agent.
7. http://www.nationaldefensemagazine.org/archive/2011/december
    /pages/usgovernmentturnstocrowdsourcingforintelligence.aspx.

CHAPTER 3: LINKING IN AND LINKING OUT

1. business.linkedin.com/talent-solutions/recruiting-resources
    -tips.
2. http://strictlyautobiographical.com/2013/02/the-milano-an-ode
    -to-pepperidge-farm.

CHAPTER 5: MIRROR, MIRROR, ON THE WALL

1. http://www.telegraph.co.uk/news/uknews/9959026/Mothers
    -asked-nearly-300-questions-a-day-study-finds.html.

CHAPTER 6: CROWD CREATIVITY

1. http://archive.wired.com/wired/archive/14.06/crowds.html.

CHAPTER 8: SMART MONEY

1. https://www.javelinstrategy.com/brochure/276.
2. https://s3.amazonaws.com/static.billguard.com/report
    /BillGuard_-_2013_Grey_Charge_Report.pdf.
3. Burton G. Malkiel, *A Random Walk Down Wall Street: The Time-
    Tested Strategy for Successful Investing* (W. W. Norton, 1973).
4. http://www.forbes.com/sites/heatherstruck/2010/10/18/can
    -twitter-predict-the-stock-market.
5. http://finance.yahoo.com/q?s=BRK-A.
6. http://www.etoro.com.

CHAPTER 9: SMILE FOR THE CROWD

1. http://www.prnewswire.com/news-releases/facebook-users
    -take-a-sharp-turn-toward-privacy-139817613.html.

2. http://www.pewinternet.org/2013/10/21/online-dating-relation ships.

3. L. Anik and M. I. Norton, "Matchmaking Promotes Happiness," *Social Psychological and Personality Science*, 1948550614522303; spp.sagepub.com/content/early/2014/02/10/1948550614522303 .full.

4. http://www.ibtimes.co.uk/lulu-app-rate-men-legal-action-brazil -528164.

5. http://www.divorce-online.co.uk/blog/social-media-is-a-factor -in-one-in-three-divorces.

6. http://www.amazon.com/The-Female-Brain-Louann-Brizendine /dp/0767920104.

7. Louann Brizendine, *The Female Brain* (Broadway Books, 2006), 37.

8. Shelley E. Taylor, et al., "Biobehavioral Responses to Stress in Females: Tend-and-Befriend, Not Fight-or-Flight," *Psychological Review* 107 (3) (2000): 411–29.

CHAPTER 10: IT TAKES A REALLY BIG VILLAGE

1. http://www.census.gov/prod/2013pubs/p20-570.pdf.

2. Ibid.

CHAPTER 11: PAGING DOCTOR CROWD

1. http://prescriptions.blogs.nytimes.com/2011/02/01/health -care-is-high-among-web-searches.

2. http://www.pewinternet.org/fact-sheets/health-fact-sheet.

3. http://www.reddit.com/r/fffffffuuuuuuuuuuuuu/comments /12kihx/pregnant_man_rage.

CHAPTER 14: DREAM A LITTLE DREAM WITH ME

1. K. R. Lorig, P. D. Mazonson, and H. R. Holman, "Evidence Suggesting That Health Education for Self-management in Patients with Chronic Arthritis Has Sustained Health Benefits While Reducing Health Care Costs," *Arthritis & Rheumatism* 36(4) (1993): 439–46.

2. D. Spiegel, et al., "Effect of Psychosocial Treatment on Survival of Patients with Metastatic Breast Cancer," *The Lancet* 334(8668) (1989): 888–91.

3. B. E. Hogan, W. Linden, and B. Najarian, "Social Support Interventions: Do They Work?," *Clinical Psychology Review* 22 (2002): 381–440, doi:10.1016/s0272-7358(01)00102-7.
4. K. P. Davison, J. W. Pennebaker, and S. S. Dickerson, "Who Talks? The Social Psychology of Illness Support Groups," *American Psychologist* 55(2) (2000): 205.

CONCLUSION: THE FUTURE OF MINDSHARING

1. http://www.eecs.harvard.edu/~kgajos/papers/2011/noronha -platemate-uist11.pdf.
2. From a presentation by Tom Boyle at the Institute for Knowledge Management Forum, Nice, France, September 1999.

INDEX